Threads of Revelation

DESTINY'S DANCE
FOOTPRINTS IN THE WILDERNESS

PAT DENIM

Reviews are important to independent authors, so if you have the time, I would really appreciate you leaving one for this book. Thank you.

Pat Denim

Threads of Revelation

DESTINY'S DANCE:
Footprints In The Wilderness

Cover Design by: Scatterling Design

Paperback: ISBN 978-1-962097-04-8
Ebook : ISBN 978-1-962097-05-5

LCCN : 2023944837

Table of Contents

TRIBE'S TALLY

In Sinai's wild, where God's voice was heard,
Within the tent where truth's flame stirred,
On the first day of month anew,
Second year since Egypt they withdrew.

"Count Israel's congregation," God commands,
Families, fathers, each in his lands.
Men of war, from twenty years and high,
Moses and Aaron shall them apply.

From each tribe a leader shall arise,
To stand with Moses, 'neath heaven's skies.
Here are their names, these noble men,
Representing each tribe, Amen.

Reuben, Simeon, Judah strong,
Issachar, Zebulun, throng by throng.
Joseph's sons, Ephraim and Manasseh bold,
Benjamin, Dan, each story told.

Asher, Naphtali, each one stands,
Princes leading, under God's commands.
Moses and Aaron, with a chosen band,
Gather the names as God has planned.

All the tribes, from twenty on,
Counted, numbered, one by one.
Reuben's tribe, forty-six thousand, five,
Simeon's number, fifty-nine thousand alive.

Gad's warriors, forty-five thousand in might,
Judah's strength, sixty-four thousand to fight.
Issachar, fifty-four thousand strong,
Zebulun, fifty-seven thousand, a throng.

Joseph's tribes, Ephraim with grace,
Forty thousand, five hundred embrace.
Manasseh follows, thirty-two and two,
Benjamin, thirty-five and four, a true crew.

Dan's numbers soar, sixty-two and seven,
Asher's tribe, forty-one thousand, leaven.
Naphtali stands at fifty-three,
Twelve tribes united, God's chosen tree.

These were the counted, Moses and more,
Leaders appointed, each tribe to explore.
Total count, a multitude grand,
Six hundred thousand, warriors stand.

Levites, God's priests, were not in the mix,
To the tribe of Levi, numbers we fix.
God's commands, to Moses they heed,
Levites chosen to serve, to lead.

Over the tabernacle's sacred domain,
Vessels and offerings, they maintain.
Bearing its weight, encamping with care,
Levites guard it, God's truth they share.

When the tabernacle moves its place,
Levites take it, with careful grace.
Pitching, setting, as needed, they strive,
Strangers beware, or you won't survive.

Each tribe's camp, with its own banner,
Orderly tents, like a well-ordered manner.
Levites encircle, with testimony's might,
Wrath avoided, Israel stays in the light.

As God decreed, His people comply,
Following His word, they amplify.
Moses and God, in unity true,
Israel obeys, God's will they pursue.

CAMPS ARRANGEMENT

Then the Lord spoke to Moses and Aaron, clear,
Each tribe shall pitch by their own banner near,
Around the tabernacle, their sacred space,
In orderly camps, they'll find their place.

Judah's banner, on the east, first to see,
With Nahshon leading, strong and free.
A host of sixty-four thousand, they stand,
Ready to follow their God's command.

Next to them, Issachar, a tribe wise,
Led by Nethaneel, under the skies.
Fifty-four thousand, their strength proclaimed,
By their banner's call, they're named.

Zebulun's tribe, by Eliab's command,
Fifty-seven thousand, ready to stand.
All under their banners, each tribe so grand,
In Judah's camp, they find their land.

Reuben's standard on the south, they reside,
Elizur their leader, by their side.
Forty-six thousand, five hundred strong,
To God's call, they all belong.

Simeon follows, Shelumiel leads the way,
Fifty-nine thousand, their count on display.
In Reuben's camp, they take their stance,
Ready to follow, in obedience.

Gad's trbe comes next, with Eliasaph bold,
Forty-five thousand, six hundred, we're told.
Their banner high, their pride they show,
In Reuben's ranks, they gladly go.

The Levites, God's chosen, midst the camp stay,
Guiding the tabernacle, day by day.
Set forth as God commands, they move in sync,
Ensuring the tabernacle's link.

Ephraim's banner waves on the west,
With Elishama leading, they are blessed.
Forty thousand, five hundred in their ranks,
In unity, their loyalty stands.

Beside them, Manasseh, by Gamaliel's reign,
Thirty-two thousand, two hundred, no disdain.
Under Ephraim's banner, they move along,
In God's plan, they all belong.

Benjamin's tribe, with Abidan their guide,
Thirty-five thousand, four hundred, side by side.
With Ephraim's camp, they march with pride,
In unity, they stride.

Dan's banner on the north, unfurled,
Ahiezer leads, around the world.
Sixty-two thousand, seven hundred strong,
In Dan's camp, they all belong.

Asher's tribe, by Pagiel led with care,
Forty-one thousand, five hundred, there.
Under Dan's banner, they march along,
A united tribe, standing strong.

Naphtali follows, Ahira's command,
Fifty-three thousand, four hundred, a united band.
In Dan's camp, they find their space,
Moving forward, they embrace.

The complete tally, under each tribe's flag,
Six hundred thousand, with thirty-five thousand tagged.
The Levites, chosen by God's design,
Set apart and obedient, in His word they align.

Israel's children, as God has said,
Pitched by their banners, no detail unspread.
Moved and marched, by their father's line,
Unified and strong, in God's design.

STRANGE FIRE

These are the generations of Aaron and Moses,
Whom God chose and spoke to, moments so close.
Aaron had four sons, as the names do reveal,
Nadab, Abihu, Eleazar, Ithamar, their zeal.

Anointed priests they were, consecrated to serve,
In the priestly office, their purpose they preserve.
Nadab and Abihu met a tragic fate,
Offered strange fire, sealed their dangerous state.

In the wilderness of Sinai, their lives they lost,
Eleazar and Ithamar continued at any cost.
The Levites God chose, a sacred tribe,
To minister to Aaron, their role imbibe.

Their charge to keep, the congregation's way,
By the tabernacle, their service to display.
All instruments, their duty to maintain,
Given to Aaron's care, a sacred domain.

Given wholly to Aaron, the Levites shall be,
No strangers allowed, for they hold the key.
Aaron and his sons, their priestly role obey,
And anyone who nears, a high price must pay.

The Levites chosen, instead of firstborn's place,
God's plan for redemption, by His grace.
For God claims all firstborn, as His own,
Since Egypt's night of sorrow, that's known.

Males from a month old, and upwards they count,
Levites take their place, God's plan to amount.
Gershon, Kohath, Merari, names distinct,
Levites' families and duties linked.

Gershon's family, with Libni and Shimei's name,
Seven thousand five hundred, in their fame.
Pitching west of the tabernacle's domain,
Under Eliasaph's leadership, they remain.

Kohath's family, Amram, Izehar, Hebron, Uzziel's line,
Eight thousand six hundred, God's call they sign.
Southward they pitch, by the tabernacle's side,
Elizaphan leads, their duty to guide.

The charge of the sanctuary, they will keep,
Ark, table, candlestick, their care is deep.
Eleazar oversees them, the chief's role is clear,
Keeping the sanctuary's charge, year after year.

Merari's family, Mahli and Mushi known,
Six thousand two hundred, God's work they've shown.
Pitching north, by the tabernacle's view,
Under Zuriel's command, they remain true.

Eastward, before the tabernacle's site,
Moses, Aaron, and sons, their duty's light.
Protecting Israel's charge, the sanctuary's grace,
Strangers who approach, God's wrath they'll face.

Twenty-two thousand Levites, as God's command,
Males from a month old, their ranks expand.
To redeem firstborn, God's plan unfolds,
Levites instead of them, His story told.

A thousand three hundred sixty-five shekels in sum,
The redemption money given, God's will is done.
For the Levites, a chosen tribe so true,
They belong to the Lord, their service they pursue.

ASSIGNED DUTIES

Gather 'round, my friend, a story to unfold,
Of Levites and their tasks, in days of old.
Kohath's sons, aged thirty to fifty, true,
Carried holy items, a sacred crew.

Covering the Ark with its vail of grace,
With blue and badger skins, in their rightful place.
Table and bread, covered with blue so bright,
The holy setup, a wondrous sight.

The candlestick too, with its lamps to ignite,
Clothed in blue, its brilliance taking flight.
Altar of gold, covered in blue array,
With badger skins to protect and display.

Their duty done, Aaron's kin take the lead,
Kohathites step back, in reverence they heed.
Now Eleazar, Aaron's son, takes his stand,
Keeper of the light, the anointing so grand.

The Levites of Gershon, age thirty to fifty,
Bore curtains and hangings, oh so nifty.
Courtyard adornments, they held with care,
A vital role, in the sacred air.

Moses and Aaron, and chiefs of the land,
Numbered Gershon's sons, a diligent band.
Merari's descendants, likewise in their prime,
Thirty to fifty, they served through time.

Boards and bars, pillars and cords,
Their burdens were many, their service records.
Aaron and his sons, with wisdom so keen,
Assigned these Levites, their duties serene.

Two thousand seven hundred, Gershon's proud kin,
With purpose they served, each thread and pin.
Merari's tribe, with three thousand and two,
Their task of service, they faithfully knew.

Eight thousand five hundred, all Levites combined,
Counted and chosen, their roles well defined.
Through ages and duties, their mission held strong,
Levites of honor, to whom we belong.

DEFILEMENT

If a leper or one unclean you find,
Out of the camp, they must be assigned.
Male or female, no matter the gender,
Outside the camp, they must surrender.

To keep the camp pure where I reside,
Their presence outside, we must decide.
Israel followed, as the Lord did decree,
Removing those unclean, setting them free.

Now, a tale of trespass and guilt I share,
When a man or woman strays, beware.
Confession and recompense must be made,
A fifth part added to what's repaid.

If no kin to receive, then to the Lord,
Compensation given, as His Word is stored.
Holy offerings, to the priest shall flow,
A portion set aside, a truth to know.

Should a wife betray, a secret sin,
Her guilt or innocence, we must begin.
A test of jealousy, a ritual to unveil,
The truth of her actions, this will entail.

Holy water mixed with tabernacle floor,
A priest's solemn charge, a sacred chore.
If she's innocent, then no curse to bear,
But if guilty, a curse she'll declare.

Drinking bitter water, the verdict is known,
If guilty, her body will be shown.
With offerings waved before the Lord's face,
The truth is revealed in this sacred space.

If defiled, her body will show the sign,
Swelling belly, rotting thigh, a clear design.
If pure, she'll conceive, a blessed sign,
God's law of jealousies, in this, we align.

So remember this law of jealousy true,
The Lord's wisdom and justice shining through.
Guilt or innocence, His light will reveal,
In every heart, His truth will heal.

VOW OF SEPARATION

Listen, Israel, and hear what I say,
Of vows of Nazarite, I convey.
Man or woman, who seeks to part,
To consecrate to Me, in heart.

From wine and strong drink they must abstain,
No grapes in any form they'll gain.
No razor shall touch their head, you see,
Let their hair grow, untouched and free.

During their vow, from death they must stay,
No defilement near, come what may.
Not even for kin shall they be unclean,
For God's consecration on them is seen.

A sudden death near, defiles their way,
On the seventh day, their hair they'll sway.
Two birds to the priest, they must bring,
Sin offering and burnt offering.

A lamb, a trespass offering to bear,
Their days of vow now seem unfair.
When their vow's complete, to the door they'll go,
Offerings for Me, they'll bestow.

A lamb and an ewe, pure and fine,
A ram for peace, in line with Mine.
Unleavened bread, wafers so neat,
Meat and drink offerings, a feast complete.

The priest shall wave them, offerings held high,
Before the Lord, with the deepest sigh.
The Nazarite's hair, the fire will take,
A sign of devotion, for My name's sake.

The priest's wave offering, a holy sight,
And then the Nazarite can enjoy the night.
This is the law for those who vow,
A life apart, My blessings they'll know.

Now, Aaron and his sons, hear Me bless,
With words of love and tenderness.
May the Lord bless and keep you tight,
May His face shine, a radiant light.

His grace be upon you, gentle and true,
May He lift His countenance, peace renew.
His name on you placed, His blessings will come,
Israel, rest assured, under His loving sum.

WHISPERS OF PRINCES

When Moses had set the tabernacle high,
Anointed and sanctified it nigh,
The instruments, the altar, all,
Both vessels great and vessels small,

Princes of Israel, heads of their kin,
Brought their offerings with hearts akin.
Six wagons covered, oxen twelve they gave,
To serve within, the sacred way to pave.

Before the Lord, the tabernacle's door,
Their offerings stood, each one to adore.
Moses heard the Lord's voice anew,
Commanding what these gifts should do.

"Use these for service," the Lord did say,
"To Levites, each according to their way."
Moses followed and did as told,
To Levites, wagons and oxen he unrolled.

Two wagons, four oxen for Gershon's clan,
In line with their service, as God's plan.
Four wagons, eight oxen for Merari's kin,
Delivered by Moses, with a faithful grin.

No wagons for Kohath's devoted throng,
Upon their shoulders they'll bear along.
The princes offered, their gifts displayed,
Anointed the altar, devotion portrayed.

On each day, a prince did come forth,
With offerings laid, east, west, south, and north.
Nahshon, Nethaneel, Eliab, too,
Elizur, Shelumiel, the chosen few.

Eliasaph, Elishama, Gamaliel next,
Each prince did follow, as the law's text.
Abidan, Ahiezer, Pagiel as well,
Offerings for dedication, in rhythm they fell.

The altar's dedication, a precious sight,
Silver chargers, bowls, and spoons of gold's light.
The silver, two thousand and four hundred it bore,
Gold spoons, one hundred and twenty, and more.

The offerings given, the altar aligned,
Burnt offerings, sin offerings, in peace combined.
Twenty-four oxen, and rams as well,
To honor the Lord, their offerings swell.

In the tabernacle, Moses heard,
A voice from above, from cherubim stirred.
From the mercy seat, the Lord spoke clear,
Guiding His people, ever near.

GUIDING LIGHT'S GLOW

The Lord spoke to Moses, clear and bright,
"Speak to Aaron, shed guiding light.
When you light the lamps, take heed,
Seven lamps shall shine, a blessed creed."

Aaron obeyed, as the Lord's voice led,
Lit the lamps as the Lord had said.
The candlestick, a work of gold so fine,
Crafted as shown, with patterns divine.

The Levites, chosen from Israel's seed,
Cleansed they must be, their hearts freed.
With water of purifying, cleanse each soul,
Shave their flesh, clothes wash, a sacred goal.

Offer a bullock for sin, pure and young,
Fine flour mingled with oil among.
Another bullock, a sin offering true,
Atonement made as commands construe.

Gather the Levites, assembly wide,
Israel's hands upon them, side by side.
Aaron offers them, an offering true,
To serve the Lord, their duty to pursue.

Lay hands on bullocks, the offerings stand,
One for sin, the other as planned.
Make atonement for Levites so dear,
Before Aaron and sons, their purpose clear.

Levites are chosen, distinct and true,
Set apart from the Israelite crew.
To serve the Lord's work, they are mine,
Replacing the firstborn, a sacred sign.

All firstborn are the Lord's, both beast and man,
Sanctified since Egypt's firstborn began.
Levites replace them, chosen and blest,
Gifted to Aaron's line, serving's quest.

Levites are set to cleanse the way,
In tabernacle's service, they'll stay.
Purified and washed, an offering pure,
Atoned by Aaron, their mission sure.

Levites step forth, the service to fulfill,
In the tabernacle's duties, a sacred skill.
As Moses was told, they followed through,
A sacred calling, they'll always pursue.

From twenty-five, their service they'll start,
In the tabernacle, they'll play their part.
Until fifty, their duties shine bright,
Then a change comes, as day turns to night.

They'll serve no more, their work is done,
But with their brethren, unity won.
They'll guard and keep, in sacred charge,
A life of service, a mission large.

OBEDIENCE TO THE CLOUD

In Sinai's wilderness, the Lord spoke anew,
In the second year, His message true.
After leaving Egypt's land behind,
The appointed Passover in their hearts entwined.

On the fourteenth day of the first month's grace,
With rites and ceremonies, they embraced.
Moses shared God's words with Israel's kin,
Urging them the Passover's path to begin.

In the wilderness of Sinai's expanse,
They kept the Passover, a sacred dance.
As God had commanded, they followed His lead,
Every detail followed, in thought and deed.

Yet certain men were defiled, you see,
By contact with death, they couldn't partake free.
They approached Moses and Aaron with plea,
"Why are we denied, from this offering to be?"

Moses said, "Wait, and let the Lord decide,
What's right for you, in this matter wide."
The Lord's voice came to Moses's ear,
Guidance divine, crystal clear.

To those unclean or distant in roam,
A chance was given, a second home.
On the fourteenth day of the next month's night,
They could keep the feast, shining bright.

With bitter herbs and unleavened bread,
The Passover's customs they still spread.
None should remain till morning light,
Or break its bones in sight.

The clean who neglected, sin would bear,
Cut off from the people, a weight to share.
If a stranger joined, seeking the Lord's grace,
The same rule applied in this holy place.

As the tabernacle rose in the air,
A cloud covered it with utmost care.
By day, the cloud's shade did stay,
By night, fire's glow led the way.

When the cloud lifted from the tent so grand,
Israel journeyed, as God's command.
Where the cloud stood, they pitched their tents,
Guided by God's divine intents.

At the Lord's command, they journeyed on,
Cloud's presence told them, night to dawn.
Whether days were few or many a year,
They abode or journeyed, God's voice clear.

By Moses's hand, the Lord's command was kept,
In tents they rested or onward stepped.
The cloud, God's guidance, they did trace,
Obeying each word, seeking His grace.

TRUMPET'S CALL

The Lord spoke again to Moses's ear,
"Craft silver trumpets, make them clear.
From a single piece, they shall be made,
For assembly calls and camps' parade."

With trumpet's sound, the assembly shall convene,
At the tabernacle door, a sight serene.
One trumpet's call gathers princes near,
Heads of thousands, those to revere.

A single alarm signals the eastern force,
Onward they go, guided by its course.
A second alarm sounds, the southern brigade,
On their journey, as plans are laid.

But when the congregation should unite,
Trumpet calls, a different plight.
Sons of Aaron shall blow the silver horn,
An eternal ordinance, since the day they were born.

In times of warfare, when foes oppress,
Sound the trumpet, their prayers to address.
God's remembrance shall shield from strife,
Saving His people, guarding their life.

In gladness, solemnity, or the month's birth,
Over offerings, sounds trumpet's mirth.
A memorial to God, to hold in mind,
"I am the Lord," His voice we find.

On the twentieth day, month two's embrace,
From the tabernacle, the cloud did erase.
Israel journeyed, following His decree,
From Sinai's desert, their path set free.

First, Judah's banner led the way,
Nahshon's guidance in the light of day.
Issachar and Zebulun, a steadfast line,
Following leaders divine.

Reuben's camp next, with Elizur at helm,
Simeon and Gad, their ranks overwhelm.
Kohathites bore the sanctuary true,
As Merari moved, the tabernacle they knew.

Ephraim, led by Elishama's light,
Manasseh and Benjamin, a united sight.
Dan's camp, the rear guard, stood tall,
Their journey guided, they answered the call.

To Hobab, Moses spoke a plea,
"Come with us, and goodness you'll see.
God's blessings await, for Israel's sake,
Guide us through this journey we undertake."

But Hobab declined, to his own land he'd wend,
Moses urged him, a plea to extend.
"Be our eyes, help us through the night,
What goodness God grants, share in our sight."

Departing the mount, three days they trod,
The ark led the way, guided by God.
By day, the cloud on them did rest,
A guardian presence, a blessed crest.

When the ark moved, Moses cried in the air,
"Rise, O Lord, let foes beware!
Scatter those who hate Thy name,
Before Thy might, let them not remain."

At rest, Moses called, a prayer sincere,
"Return, O Lord, draw near, draw near.
To Israel's multitudes, favor extend,
Guide us on this journey, till journey's end."

FIERY LESSON

The people's complaints, a bitter sound,
Reached the Lord's ear, His anger unbound.
A fire from Him raged through the camp,
Consuming those who dared to tamp.

Moses interceded, to the Lord he prayed,
The fire quenched, the destruction stayed.
The place named Taberah, a mark of the blaze,
Where God's fiery anger did amaze.

A mixed multitude, a lustful cry,
Israel wept for flesh, to the sky.
They longed for the food of Egypt's land,
Fish, cucumbers, leeks, a menu grand.

But their souls grew weak, as manna they ate,
Nothing but this, their daily plate.
Coriander-like, its form and hue,
Manna, heaven-sent, a faithful view.

They gathered and ground, they baked and made,
Manna transformed, a daily aid.
The taste like fresh oil, a flavor pure,
Manna sustained them, God's love sure.

At night, dew fell, manna came down,
A heavenly gift, a holy crown.
Yet the people wept by their tent's door,
God's anger stirred, His patience wore.

Moses cried, "Why afflict me so?
Burdened by their cries, to and fro.
Shall I bear them like a father's hold?
This weight upon me, so hard to mold."

The Lord replied, "Gather elders true,
Seventy strong, I'll bestow on you.
My spirit upon them, they'll share your task,
Helping you lead, the burden unmask."

Sanctify yourselves, the Lord then told,
Tomorrow, flesh your desires shall unfold.
For your weeping and longing for the past,
Flesh I'll provide, your request amassed.

Not for a day, or ten, or twenty more,
But a month of flesh, a plentiful store.
Yet with loathing, you'll see and learn,
Despising the Lord, who brought your turn.

Moses doubted, questioned the means,
Could God satisfy their daily glean?
But the Lord's hand is never weak,
His word always true, the future He'll speak.

Moses gathered seventy, elders in sight,
Around the tabernacle, bathed in light.
God's spirit on them, they prophesied so,
Guided by His power, His wisdom to show.

Eldad and Medad, in the camp remained,
God's spirit on them, their voices unchained.
Word reached Moses, a young man's voice,
Eldad and Medad, they too rejoice.

Joshua worried, their actions he defied,
Moses spoke, "Would all were prophesied!
Let God's spirit on all His people rest,
To prophesy and lead, be they blessed."

The Lord sent a wind, from the sea quails flew,
A feast for the people, a skyward view.
But their greed consumed, as the quails fell,
God's wrath ignited, a painful spell.

Before the meat was chewed, His anger broke,
A plague surged forth, a heavy yoke.
They buried the lusters, a name they gave,
Kibroth-hattaavah, a lustful grave.

From Kibroth-hattaavah, they onward pressed,
To Hazeroth they went, their journey's quest.

VISIONS AND DREAMS

Against Moses, Miriam and Aaron spoke,
A complaint about his wife, a doubt they awoke.
He had wed an Ethiopian, it's told,
Their concern for this union took hold.

"Has the Lord not spoken through us?" they questioned,
Their own authority, they mentioned.
The Lord heard their words, His response was clear,
A divine message, they were about to hear.

Moses, meek above all on earth's vast plains,
God's chosen prophet, amid life's strains.
The Lord summoned them three, to the tabernacle's site,
Where He revealed His power, His might.

In a pillar of cloud, the Lord descended,
To Aaron and Miriam, His will He intended.
He spoke of Moses, His faithful guide,
A prophet who walked by His side.

Through visions and dreams, God spoke to some,
But Moses was different, God's chosen one.
With Moses, the Lord conversed face to face,
A unique connection, a divine embrace.

God's anger flared against Aaron and Miriam's speech,
Their disrespect for Moses, a lesson to teach.
The cloud departed, Miriam's skin turned pale,
Leprous white, her appearance frail.

Aaron pleaded, "Forgive us our sin,
For foolishness and wrong we've been in."
Moses cried out to the Lord on her behalf,
"Please heal her," he pleaded, feeling her pain's half.

God spoke again, a seven-day wait,
For Miriam's healing, her repentance's date.
Shut out from the camp, her sin to mend,
A time of reflection, her ways to amend.

Seven days passed, the people did wait,
Until Miriam's return, they could not abate.
They journeyed from Hazeroth, toward a new dawn,
The wilderness of Paran, their path drawn.

IN THE EYES OF GIANTS

The Lord to Moses then did say,
"Send forth men to Canaan's way,
From each tribe a ruler's hand,
To explore the land, as I command."

Moses chose leaders, by God's decree,
Twelve in all, a company.
From Reuben to Gad, the tribes were named,
To spy the land, they were proclaimed.

Off they went, a mission to fulfill,
From Zin's wilderness, to distant hill.
Hebron they reached, where giants dwelled,
Anak's children, their strength compelled.

They cut a branch with clusters fair,
Grapes and figs they brought to share.
The brook of Eshcol, its name derived,
From grapes they cut and brought alive.

Forty days they searched the land,
Then returned to their people's band.
To Moses, Aaron, and the crowd they showed,
The fruitful land, its bounty bestowed.

"We've reached the land," they gladly said,
"Milk and honey's here," their voices spread.
But they also shared a cautious tale,
Of mighty foes and walls that impale.

Amalekites, Hittites, foes all around,
Canaan's dwellers, walled and sound.
Anak's children, giants in sight,
Their fears ignited, day and night.

Caleb rose, with courage anew,
"Let's conquer the land, for we are true!"
But some disagreed, their hearts with fear,
"We can't prevail, the danger's clear."

An evil report, they did proclaim,
Of the land they'd seen, a land of fame.
"Devours its people," they did claim,
Giants and foes, a land of shame.

With eyes of grasshoppers, they saw,
In giants' sight, weak and in awe.
Fearful hearts, their courage did wane,
Doubted their strength, and faced disdain.

FRUSTRATING GOD

The people lifted up their voice in cries,
Weeping through the night, with troubled eyes.
Against Moses and Aaron, murmurs arose,
Longing for Egypt, where they once were close.

"Why lead us here to meet our doom,
To fall by swords and face our gloom?
Better in Egypt or wilderness to dwell,
Than in this land where dangers swell."

"Let's choose a leader, return we must,
Back to Egypt, where life we trust."
Moses and Aaron fell upon their face,
Before the assembly, in humble grace.

Joshua and Caleb, with clothes they tore,
Spoke to the people, their faith they bore.
The land is good, they boldly said,
God is with us, fear not, be not misled.

Rebellion brewed, the crowd turned cold,
A stoning threat, their anger bold.
But the Lord's glory appeared on high,
In the tabernacle, before their eye.

The Lord said to Moses, His voice was stern,
"How long will they doubt and never learn?
With pestilence I shall smite them now,
A greater nation from you I'll endow."

Moses pleaded, "What will they say?
Egypt will mock, their doubts will sway.
Show Your mercy, forgive their sin,
Proclaim Your glory, let hope begin."

The Lord pardoned, as Moses pled,
His mercy prevailing, love widespread.
But the consequence, a solemn truth,
Forty years of wandering, no land's booth.

Caleb's faith stood, a spirit strong,
He and Joshua, the faithful throng,
Shall enter the land, a future grand,
The rest shall fall, in the desert sand.

Moses told the people the words divine,
They mourned, they wept, in somber line.
They rose early, to the mountain they went,
Promised to conquer, but God's intent

Was clear and firm, their way was blocked,
For Amalekites and Canaanites flocked.
In their self-will, they were denied,
The Lord's presence gone, they would not abide.

They went to the hilltop, a last display,
The Ark stayed back, they'd gone astray.
Amalekites struck, defeat was found,
Hormah's defeat on the hill's ground.

PRESUMPTUOUS DEFIANCE

The Lord spoke to Moses anew,
Guiding His people in what to do.
When in the land of their habitation,
Offerings to Him, a sweet dedication.

For burnt offerings and solemn feasts,
A tenth of flour, oil for the feasts.
A drink offering too, sweet to the Lord,
A pleasing aroma, an act adored.

Lambs, rams, and bullocks they would bring,
A choice offering for their God, their King.
Wine poured as well, a sweet delight,
A pleasing sacrifice, in God's sight.

Born of the country, or a stranger true,
One law for all, the same for the two.
Heave offerings given, of bread they eat,
Acknowledging God's gifts so sweet.

Yet if mistakes were made in the way,
A bullock and goat as atonement lay.
The priest intercedes, an offering made,
Forgiveness granted, sins washed, displayed.

But deliberate sin, a soul's reproach,
Cut off from the people, God's righteous approach.
Despising His word, His commands denied,
Iniquity remains, a weight they can't hide.

In the wilderness, a man gathering wood,
On the Sabbath day, as he understood.
They brought him to Moses, his fate unsure,
The Lord's command came, justice pure.

Stoned outside the camp, his life it ceased,
A lesson in obedience, a warning for the least.
Fringes on garments, a visual guide,
Remember God's commands, in Him confide.

A blue ribbon on the fringes to be,
A reminder of God's law, His decree.
Seek not your heart's desires, be pure,
Follow God's ways, His path secure.

"I am the lord your god," he proclaimed,
Who from Egypt's land, you I reclaimed.
Obey My commands, be holy and true,
I am your God, who guides and renews."

FIERY CONSEQUENCE

Korah, Dathan, Abiram, and their crew,
Against Moses and Aaron they grew.
Two hundred fifty, renowned and bold,
Rose against them, a story to be told.

Claiming too much power the leaders possess,
Holy is the congregation, their address.
Moses fell on his face, humble and true,
Awaiting the Lord's judgment to come through.

A test of censers, incense, and flame,
Tomorrow the Lord would reveal His name.
Korah and his group, take censers in hand,
Before the Lord, a trial they'd withstand.

Moses warned of the danger they faced,
Rebelling against God, they'd be erased.
The earth might open, swallowing them whole,
A sign of God's judgment, taking its toll.

Yet Dathan and Abiram resisted the call,
Refusing to come, their pride standing tall.
Accusing Moses of arrogance they said,
Bringing them out to die, they dread.

Moses angered by their defiance so clear,
Warned of the consequences they must adhere.
The Lord would reveal if Moses was right,
A unique fate awaited them that night.

The ground beneath them opened wide,
Swallowing them in, a terrible tide.
Their households, their goods, all consumed by earth,
Divine judgment declared, sealing their worth.

A fire from the Lord consumed the rest,
Two hundred fifty, put to the test.
The Lord spoke again to Moses, be clear,
Tell Eleazar to save censers so dear.

A covering for the altar, a memorial grand,
A lesson to all throughout the land.
No stranger shall offer incense and stand,
Lest they face the same fate, as the Lord had planned.

But the people of Israel continued to complain,
Blaming Moses and Aaron for the pain.
The cloud covered the tabernacle, divine display,
Moses and Aaron, before it they'd pray.

The Lord's wrath was unleashed, a plague began,
Aaron swiftly intervened, following God's plan.
Atonement he made, between death and life,
Stopping the plague, calming the strife.

Fourteen thousand seven hundred had died,
From the plague's rampage, none could hide.
Aaron's action halted the deathly tide,
Returning to Moses, God's mercy their guide.

HUSHED MURMURS

The Lord's voice reached Moses once more,
A solution for the quarrels He did implore.
"Take twelve rods," He instructed Moses with care,
From each tribe's leader, a rod they would bear.

Upon each rod, the leader's name to write,
A sign to end their continuous fight.
On Levi's rod, inscribed Aaron's name,
A choice to quell the discontent's flame.

In the tabernacle, the rods were placed,
Before the Lord's presence, they were embraced.
A test to determine the chosen one,
Whose rod would blossom, under God's sun.

The following day, as Moses did seek,
In the tabernacle, his spirit so meek,
Aaron's rod of Levi, a sight to behold,
Budded, blossomed, and almonds it told.

All the rods were brought out for all to see,
Each man claimed his rod with glee.
But the Lord spoke again to Moses, be clear,
Take Aaron's rod as a token, bring it near.

For the rebels who murmur, against Me they stand,
This rod will remind them of My command.
The people were filled with fear and dread,
As the consequence of their actions they read.

The lesson was clear, as the rod did attest,
Approach the Lord's sanctuary with reverence, not jest.
Death would follow those who were impure,
A solemn reminder for all to endure.

The people cried out, overwhelmed with despair,
Afraid of the danger, the weight they couldn't bear.
Approaching the Lord's presence, a serious matter,
Respecting His holiness, their lives they'd flatter.

CHOSEN ROD

The Lord spoke to Aaron, making it clear,
The iniquities of the sanctuary, they would bear.
Aaron and his sons, the priesthood's weight they'd share,
For service in God's presence, a sacred affair.

The tribe of Levi, brethren of Aaron's line,
Would join in service, a role so divine.
To minister before the tabernacle's door,
Yet not approach the holy vessels any more.

No stranger would come near, on this they agreed,
Death would be the consequence, a solemn creed.
The Levites were chosen, a gift to the Lord,
To serve in the tabernacle, His work to afford.

A priestly office for Aaron and his seed,
An everlasting covenant, a holy creed.
The best of offerings, the hallowed, the pure,
Reserved for the priesthood, a gift to ensure.

The firstfruits and tithes, a covenant of salt,
For Aaron and his lineage, a sacred vault.
No earthly inheritance, God was their share,
His presence, their portion, beyond compare.

For the Levites, the tithes from Israel's hand,
An offering to the Lord, a sacred command.
A heave offering to Aaron, a portion to give,
From the people's tithes, their service to relive.

A reward for their labor, they'd eat in delight,
In every place they dwelled, day and night.
No sin would they bear, their offering pure,
Lest they defile God's gifts, and His wrath endure.

RITUAL OF DEFILEMENT

The Lord spoke again, His commands to declare,
Regarding the red heifer, a process to prepare.
A spotless, unblemished cow, yoke it never bore,
A symbol of purity, as the law did implore.

Give her to Eleazar, the priest pure and true,
Outside the camp, a sacrifice, this is what you must do.
Before his face, she'll be slain, her blood to spread,
Before the tabernacle, seven times, it's said.

Her skin, her flesh, her blood, her dung, all must burn,
In the sight of all, a lesson to learn.
With cedar wood, hyssop, and scarlet, combined,
Cast into the fire, a purification sign.

The priest shall wash his clothes, bathe in water as well,
Then he can enter the camp, this story to tell.
The one who burns the cow, he, too, must be clean,
Wash his clothes, bathe in water, as it is foreseen.

A clean man shall gather the ashes with care,
Lay them outside the camp, in a clean place to bear.
A water of separation, for Israel's use it's stored,
Purification from sin, through this symbol of the Lord.

Who gathers the ashes, stays unclean in this span,
Till evening, his clothes washed, according to plan.
A touch to the dead brings seven days' uncleanness,
But the cleansing process exceeds such brief meanness.

One who touches death but neglects the right way,
Defiles God's dwelling, impure in display.
Severed from his people, this soul shall remain,
Without water of cleansing, uncleanness will gain.

When death occurs within a tent's embrace,
Seven days' impurity takes its place.
Open vessels, uncovered, tainted shall be,
Contamination spreads through touch, clearly to see.

With running water and ashes, purity shall come,
On the third and seventh day, cleaning for some.
Sprinkled on the tent, its contents, one and all,
This process of cleansing answers the call.

But neglecting the rite, remaining unclean,
Cut off from the congregation, as the Lord did mean.
A perpetual statute, this purification's grace,
He who sprinkles the water, must wash in its embrace.

Whatever the unclean touches, unclean it becomes,
Until evening's approach, until the day's sum.
A lesson in purity, defilement's grip,
A reminder to honor God's commands, not let them slip.

MOUNT HOR'S DECREE

In Zin's desert vast, as the month began,
The congregation gathered, finding their span.
In Kadesh, Miriam found her resting space,
Her death marked that moment, a somber embrace.

Water scarce and complaints arose from their heart,
Moses and Aaron faced their verbal dart.
"Why did you bring us here, to perish and thirst?"
In frustration, their doubts and anger burst.

"Is this wilderness fate, where life fades away?
Cattle and people, all will decay.
Unfit for us, this barren expanse,
Our complaints and fears, in the air they dance."

Before the tent's door, Moses and Aaron fell,
Imploring God's guidance, their voices to swell.
Radiant glory appeared, lighting the scene,
Dispelling the darkness, revealing the unseen.

"Take your rod," the Lord said, "gather all to me,
Speak to the rock, and water you'll see.
From the rock, it shall flow, a life-giving stream,
For people and cattle, a fulfilling dream."

Moses, with his rod, faced the gathered throng,
His voice firm, rebuking rebellion so strong.
"Listen, you rebels!" his words echoed wide,
Striking the rock twice, water gushed inside.

Water flowed abundantly, quenching their thirst,
In the desert's dryness, its blessing dispersed.
Yet the Lord's voice returned, a stern, clear reproof,
"Moses, you lacked faith," a solemn truth.

For Moses struck twice, not as the Lord told,
A consequence grave, a story to unfold.
The Promised Land denied, a journey unfulfilled,
Disobedience's fruit, their future chilled.

Meribah's water, a reminder it'd be,
Of strife with the Lord, disobedience free.
From Kadesh, they moved, to Hor's mountain high,
A new chapter written, as Aaron would fly.

On Hor's mount, God spoke, Moses' heart heavy,
Aaron's earthly journey ending, a legacy.
He'd not see the land that the Lord did show,
For Meribah's moment, the future's flow.

Eleazar, Aaron's son, took up the lead,
On Hor's summit's peak, where hearts did bleed.
Mourning for thirty days, a nation in sorrow,
Aaron's memory lived on, today and tomorrow.

Aaron's service and life, a flame that would burn,
A chapter concluded, a lesson to discern.

VICTORY OVER OG

In the desert wild and free,
A tale of old, I'll share with thee.
King Arad, Canaan's might,
Heard of our approach, a fearsome sight.

He fought against us, fierce and bold,
Took prisoners, stories to be told.
With a vow, we turned to God above,
Promising to conquer, cities to remove.

The Lord listened, granted our plea,
Delivered Canaan's lands, victory decree.
Mount Hor left behind, a journey long,
But doubts and hardships tried to throng.

"From Egypt brought we're here to die?"
Such complaints echoed to the sky.
No bread, no water, spirits sank,
Yet fiery serpents struck, their venom rank.

We cried, "We've sinned," to Moses true,
Praying for serpents' end, a hopeful cue.
A serpent of brass on a pole so high,
Look, and you'll live, no need to die.

Onward we traveled, to Oboth's space,
Ijeabarim, Zared's valley embrace.
To Arnon's side, we made our way,
Moab's border marked, where we'd stay.

"In wars of old," a book did say,
Red Sea's tale, Arnon's brook's display.
We came to Beer, a well so sweet,
A song of thanks our voices greet.

Princes dug, nobles with their staves,
Guided by God, no less than braves.
From Mattanah to Nahaliel's grace,
To Bamoth's heights, our steps did trace.

Bamoth led us to Moab's view,
Pisgah's top, a sight so true.
To Sihon, Amorite king, we sent,
"Let us pass," our message meant.

Yet Sihon's heart was harsh and stern,
Against us, his people did he turn.
At Jahaz's fields, we stood our ground,
A battle fierce, victory profound.

Sihon fell, his rule undone,
From Arnon to Jabbok, battles won.
Amorite cities, Heshbon's might,
In our grasp, a triumph bright.

"Come to Heshbon," a saying spread,
Fire and flame, Ar's lords, now fled.
Moab's woes, a captive's plight,
Sihon's reign, a darkened light.

Og, king of Bashan, next in line,
Spies went forth, a mission fine.
Villages taken, Amorites in flight,
Og met his end, our conquering right.

Fear not, said the Lord to me,
For victory's thine, as you'll see.
Og and his people, defeated strong,
Land taken, our journey prolonged.

In this tale of battles grand,
Through wilderness, our feet did stand.
Challenges faced, victories won,
Our journey's tale, under the sun.

TALKING ASS

In Moab's plains, by Jordan's side,
The Israelites did now abide.
Balak, Moab's king, did fear their might,
For they had conquered in many a fight.

Moab worried, distressed they stood,
Thinking our people's power was good.
To the elders of Midian they went,
Saying, "They'll devour us, they're so immense!"

Balak, the Moabite king of the time,
Sent for Balaam, skilled in the divine.
To Pethor by the river's shore,
He called Balaam, seeking to implore.

"Israel's come, from Egypt's land,
Vast as the sand, covering the strand.
Curse them, Balaam," Balak's plea,
"Perhaps we'll conquer, set us free."

So, Balaam was summoned, a tempting deal,
Riches and honor, Balak's appeal.
But Balaam knew, his heart held fast,
He couldn't defy God's word, steadfast.

He sought the Lord's guidance, with patience to wait,
A night's rest to know his fate.
God came to him, words He spoke,
"If they call, you can go, it's not a joke."

Balaam rose with the new sun's gleam,
With Moab's princes, he joined the stream.
God's anger kindled, a challenge met,
An angel stood before him, a path to set.

The ass saw the angel, a celestial sight,
Turned from the road, veered left and right.
Balaam struck the ass, the poor creature's plight,
Thrice he hit, in his angry fight.

The angel moved, in a narrow space,
No turning left or right, no escape's embrace.
The ass fell beneath Balaam's ire,
He struck again, his patience dire.

Then the Lord opened the ass's mouth,
Words came forth, strange from the South.
"Why hurt me?" the ass asked in voice so strange,
"Three times you've hit me, it's quite deranged."

Balaam's anger blazed, his response stern,
He wished for a sword, the ass to burn.
The ass spoke more, "Am I not thine?
Ridden by you, since a youngling fine."

The Lord opened Balaam's eyes, a surprise so deep,
The angel revealed, his heart took a leap.
Balaam fell to his face in awe,
Recognizing his error, his misguided flaw.

The angel spoke, stern words did flow,
"Why smite your ass? A truth to know.
I stood in your path, to halt your quest,
Your ways are wrong, a painful test."

Balaam confessed, his sin laid bare,
The angel's purpose, now made clear.
"Go with them, but only speak my word,
Obey my voice," the angel stirred.

Balak met Balaam, in Moab's border land,
"Why delay? I called," he demanded.
"I've come," Balaam said, "I'll share what's true,
Only God's word, I shall construe."

Balak offered oxen and sheep so grand,
To Balaam and his accompanying band.
They ascended high, to see the view,
Balak's hopes rising, his plan anew.

CLASH OF INTENTIONS

"Build altars here, prepare the scene,
Seven oxen, seven rams, let them convene.
As Balaam spoke, Balak obeyed,
Each altar set, a sacrifice displayed.

"Stay by the offering, watch the fire's light,
I'll go to meet the Lord, seek insight.
His words to me, I'll surely share,
Whatever He reveals, I'll declare."

Balaam ascended to a lofty place,
Meeting God, feeling His grace.
"I've readied altars, offerings so fine,
A bullock, a ram on each shrine."

The Lord placed words upon Balaam's lips,
"Return to Balak, don't let time slip.
Speak as I instruct, follow my way,
What I put in your mouth, convey."

Balaam returned, to the altar he stood,
With princes of Moab, in a thoughtful mood.
He spoke a parable, his words took flight,
Balak's request, he'd shed some light.

"Balak, the king of Moab's domain,
From Aram's hills, you brought me, it's plain.
You sought to curse, to bring them low,
Jacob and Israel, your foes."

"But how can I curse those blessed by God,
Whom He favors, against all odds?
From mountaintops I see them rise,
Distinct, unique, under heavenly skies."

"Who can count the dust of Jacob's land,
Or the fourth part of Israel's band?
Oh, let me die as the righteous do,
May my end be like theirs, true."

Balak said, "What have you done?
To curse my foes, my chosen one?
Yet you've blessed them, how could it be?
I thought you'd help, set them free."

Balaam replied, "I speak His word,
The Lord's command is what I've heard.
Should I not heed, should I not obey,
What God has placed in my way?"

Balak urged, "Come, let's try again,
From another spot, curse them, then.
Another view, a different sight,
Maybe you can bring them plight."

To the field of Zophim, Balaam led,
Built seven altars, as God had said.
Offered bullocks and rams so true,
Prepared to seek insight anew.

Balaam said, "Stand by the fire's gleam,
Here by your offering, remain, it seems.
I'll meet the Lord, His word I'll gain,
To you, I'll tell what I ascertain."

Once more, God met Balaam's gaze,
His words upon his lips, a heavenly phrase.
To Balak's query, Balaam gave reply,
"Rise up, Balak, hear what I imply."

"God is no man, nor lies, nor repents,
His word stands true, no false pretense.
He's commanded me to bless, it's done,
And blessed they are, by the Holy One."

"In Jacob, no iniquity is found,
No perverseness in Israel's ground.
The Lord, their God, is by their side,
A king's triumphant shout, their pride."

"From Egypt's grasp, God set them free,
As strong as a unicorn, they be.
No enchantment, no spell shall sway,
Jacob and Israel, come what may."

"Like a great lion, they shall rise,
A young lion fierce, eyes set on prize.
They won't rest till the prey is caught,
The blood of the fallen, their thirst sought."

Balak urged, "Neither bless nor curse,
No words for better or worse."
But Balaam replied, as in prior rounds,
"I must obey God's voice, His bounds."

"Let's try again, a new scene to see,
Perhaps God's will will come to be."
To Peor's peak, they made their way,
Seven altars rose, offerings in display.

Balaam's voice, a familiar song,
"Build seven altars, prepare them strong."
Balak obeyed, the ritual done,
A bullock, a ram on each one.

BEYOND ENCHANTMENTS

Seeing that the Lord's blessing was clear,
Balaam refrained from his usual sphere.
No more seeking enchantments' sway,
He turned his gaze toward the wilds that lay.

Lifting his eyes, Israel he spied,
In tents by tribes, their lives abide.
The spirit of God upon him came,
Filling his heart with words aflame.

A parable formed on his lips,
Truth from a trance where vision slips.
He heard God's voice, saw visions bold,
His eyes wide open, his heart uncontrolled.

"How fair are Jacob's tents," he cried,
"Israel's abode, where they do bide.
Like valleys stretched, a garden's grace,
Trees by the riverside, a tranquil space.

"Water poured from abundant source,
Seed in many waters, a prosperous course.
Their king above Agag's height,
A kingdom rising to heavens' light.

"From Egypt's chains, God brought them clear,
Strong as a unicorn, no fear.
They'll conquer nations, foes undone,
Piercing through with arrows, battles won.

"Couched like a lion, he takes his rest,
Great as a lion, none can contest.
Blessed is the one who blesses thee,
Cursed is he who dares to decree."

Balak's wrath flared, he smote his hand,
"Called you to curse, but you've blessed the land.
Flee now from here, no honor you'll find,
The Lord's kept you from greatness, bind."

Balaam replied, "Didn't I convey,
To your messengers, what I'd obey?
Silver, gold in heaps, can't sway me so,
Only the Lord's command, I'll bestow."

"I'm off to my people, my course I chart,
I'll show you what's to come, a prophetic art.
A parable formed, my lips to confess,
A vision unveiled, the future's impress."

Again, a parable rose in his heart,
Knowledge of God's ways, a mystical art.
A Star from Jacob, a Sceptre will rise,
Smite Moab's corners, shatter false ties.

Edom and Seir, lands to be won,
Israel's valiant deeds under the sun.
Dominion shall reign from Jacob's line,
Destruction shall come, the wicked to confine.

Gazing at Amalek, his parable grew,
Once great among nations, but now he'd rue.
Kenites too, dwelling strong and stout,
Yet Asshur's capture would bring about.

"Alas," he cried, "when God's will unfolds,
Who shall endure, what tale it holds!
Ships from Chittim, to trouble they bring,
Affliction to Asshur, destruction shall sing."

Balaam departed, returned to his place,
Balak too, left in a restless pace.
The parables spoken, the visions laid bare,
A story of destiny, in the desert's air.

DECEPTIVE SCHEMES

In Shittim, Israel took their stay,
But temptation led them astray.
Daughters of Moab, allure so fair,
They succumbed to their gods' snare.

To the gods they bowed, feasted in sin,
Idolatry's trap drew them in.
Joined to Baalpeor, the Lord's ire grew,
His anger against them, strong and true.

Moses received the divine command,
"Take the leaders, a drastic stand,
Hang them before the Lord's fierce gaze,
To turn His wrath, this path we raise."

Moses spoke to judges with might,
"Strike those who embraced the idol's light.
Baalpeor's followers, take their life,
End this sinful, adulterous strife."

A man of Israel, led astray,
Brought a Midianite woman one day,
In sight of the tabernacle, they stood,
While Israel's cries to the Lord they would.

Phinehas, son of Aaron, arose,
With a javelin in hand, his zeal he shows.
Into the tent, after them he went,
Thrusting through, their lives he rent.

Thus the plague ceased, no longer spread,
Twenty-four thousand, numbered as dead.
Phinehas' zealous act caught God's eye,
His wrath turned away, no longer nigh.

God spoke to Moses, covenant of peace,
To Phinehas, His favor wouldn't cease.
Everlasting priesthood for his line,
For his fervor, for the divine.

Zimri, a Simeonite, met his end,
With Cozbi, a Midianite, condemned.
Phinehas, hero of this dire scene,
Was granted honor, his name pristine.

"Vex the Midianites," God decreed,
Their deceitful ways, their evil creed.
For Peor's sake, their sister's fate,
In the plague's wake, sealed their dire state.

THE NON-INHERITED

In Shittim, Israel took their stay,
But temptation led them astray.
Daughters of Moab, allure so fair,
They succumbed to their gods' snare.

To the gods they bowed, feasted in sin,
Idolatry's trap drew them in.
Joined to Baalpeor, the Lord's ire grew,
His anger against them, strong and true.

Moses received the divine command,
"Take the leaders, a drastic stand,
Hang them before the Lord's fierce gaze,
To turn His wrath, this path we raise."

Moses spoke to judges with might,
"Strike those who embraced the idol's light.
Baalpeor's followers, take their life,
End this sinful, adulterous strife."

A man of Israel, led astray,
Brought a Midianite woman one day,
In sight of the tabernacle, they stood,
While Israel's cries to the Lord they would.

Phinehas, son of Aaron, arose,
With a javelin in hand, his zeal he shows.
Into the tent, after them he went,
Thrusting through, their lives he rent.

Thus the plague ceased, no longer spread,
Twenty-four thousand, numbered as dead.
Phinehas' zealous act caught God's eye,
His wrath turned away, no longer nigh.

God spoke to Moses, covenant of peace,
To Phinehas, His favor wouldn't cease.
Everlasting priesthood for his line,
For his fervor, for the divine.

Zimri, a Simeonite, met his end,
With Cozbi, a Midianite, condemned.
Phinehas, hero of this dire scene,
Was granted honor, his name pristine.

"Vex the Midianites," God decreed,
Their deceitful ways, their evil creed.
For Peor's sake, their sister's fate,
In the plague's wake, sealed their dire state.

DAUGHTERS INHERITANCE

Zelophehad's daughters, courage they show,
Mahlah, Noah, Hoglah, Milcah, and Tirzah, aglow.
Before Moses and Eleazar, their plea they raise,
At the tabernacle door, seeking just ways.

"Our father has passed, his name lives on,
No sons to inherit, his legacy's gone.
Grant us his portion, his land and his share,
Let fairness prevail, let us your ruling bear."

Moses presents their case, seeking Divine reply,
God's answer comes, removing any deny.
Zelophehad's daughters shall not be denied,
In their father's inheritance, they're justified.

This law for Israel, a decree Divine,
If a man has no son, let justice align.
To daughter or brethren, the inheritance is due,
A testament of fairness, a law to construe.

To Mount Abarim, Moses' steps ascend,
The land promised to Israel, a message to send.
Like Aaron, he's called to join his kin,
Resting in peace, their journeys akin.

In Zin's desert, strife found its abode,
At Meribah's water, frustrations flowed.
Moses cried to the Lord, seeking His light,
Guidance and aid, in that arid plight.

"Appoint a leader," his plea did implore,
To guide with wisdom, to lead evermore.
A shepherd to guide, both in sun and in shade,
A pillar of strength, doubt to evade.

God's answer reached Moses, clear and divine,
Joshua, son of Nun, chosen to shine.
Lay hands upon him, with honor and might,
Leading God's people, day and night.

Before Eleazar, Joshua would stand,
Seeking God's counsel, at His command.
Guiding the people, both near and afar,
Their leader, their guide, their shining star.

Moses obeyed, as God's will did decree,
Before Eleazar and all eyes to see.
Upon Joshua's shoulders, hands gently pressed,
A charge from above, leadership blessed.

RITUALS AND RITES

Listen, children of Israel, heed this decree,
The offering, the bread, for sacrifices free,
A sweet aroma, unto Me shall arise,
In due seasons, present them before your eyes.

Two spotless lambs, first-year's pristine grace,
Daily burnt offerings, in their rightful place,
One lamb at morn, the other when day is through,
With a tenth of ephah flour, mingled with oil true.

This constant burnt offering, ordained and divine,
On Sinai's mount, My favor doth it sign,
Pour a fourth hin of strong wine for Me,
A drink offering in the holy sanctuary.

At evening, the other lamb with care,
As morning's meat offering, its scent shall share,
A fragrant fire sacrifice, pleasing and pure,
A sweet aroma rising, steadfast and sure.

On Sabbath, two lambs, young and undefiled,
With two tenth deals of flour, mingled and mild,
Their drink offering too, do not forget,
Beside the constant burnt offering's set.

At each month's start, a new offering to bring,
Two bullocks, one ram, seven lambs to sing,
Three tenth deals of flour for a bullock's grace,
Two for the ram's place, an offering to embrace.

For each lamb, a tenth deal, mingled with care,
With wine, a portion, a pleasing air,
And one goat for atonement, as is due,
An offering for redemption, pure and true.

Present these beside the morning's fire bright,
A daily feast, a celestial delight,
Throughout seven days, the aroma shall swell,
Beside the continual burnt offering's spell.

On the seventh day, gather in pure delight,
An assembly holy, a respite from fight,
And on the day of first fruits, as weeks are complete,
A new offering, an offering sweet.

Two bullocks, one ram, seven lambs shall stand,
A gift of flour mingled, with oil so grand,
Offer them, an aroma to the heavens take,
A pleasant fire sacrifice, for My sake.

Beside the continual burnt offering, they stand,
With flour offerings and drink in hand,
Without blemish, pure and true,
Follow these offerings, My children, as you do.

THE SEVENTH MONTH

In the seventh month, on the first day's dawn,
A holy convocation, no servile work to spawn,
A day of trumpet blowing, a sacred sound,
Offer a burnt offering, sweet fragrance unbound.

One young bullock, one ram, and lambs seven,
In their first year's grace, free from blemish leaven,
Their meat offering with oil, carefully prepared,
For the bullock, three tenth deals, with precision paired.

Two tenth deals for the ram, a worthy treat,
And a tenth for each lamb, an aroma so sweet,
A kid of goats for atonement, a sin offering true,
Beside the burnt offering, in a blaze of virtue.

On the tenth day, a holy convocation near,
Afflict your souls, no work, no earthly cheer,
Offer a bullock, a ram, lambs seven to find,
Without blemish, a sacrifice to bind.

Meat offering of flour with oil mingled right,
Three tenth deals for the bullock, a glorious sight,
Two tenth deals for the ram, a perfect blend,
And for each lamb, a tenth, to the end.

A kid of goats for sin offering, pure and clear,
Beside the continual burnt offering, sincere,
And on the fifteenth day, a feast divine,
Seven days, no servile work, a celebration's sign.

Offer thirteen bullocks, two rams to adore,
Fourteen lambs, a blemish-free, sacred score,
Meat offering of flour with oil combined,
Three tenth deals for each bullock, clearly defined.

Two for each ram, a pleasing array,
A tenth deal for each lamb, a tribute to pay,
A kid of goats for sin offering's embrace,
Beside the continual burnt offering's grace.

On the second day, twelve bullocks stand tall,
Two rams and lambs fourteen, hear their call,
Meat offering and drink, as their number agree,
Beside a sin offering, pure and free.

On the third day, eleven bullocks in line,
Two rams and fourteen lambs, a sight so divine,
Meat offering and drink, to their number belong,
And a goat for sin offering, to atonement prolong.

The fourth day brings ten bullocks, strong and grand,
Two rams, fourteen lambs, a sacred strand,
Meat offering and drink, to their count adhere,
And a goat for sin offering, redemption is near.

The fifth day, nine bullocks, rams two and lambs bright,
Meat offering and drink, an offering's true light,
A goat for sin offering, beside the constant fire,
Atonement's desire, rising higher and higher.

On the sixth day, eight bullocks come in view,
Two rams, and lambs fourteen, a tribute so true,
Meat offering and drink, in their proper array,
And a goat for sin offering, a solemn array.

The seventh day, seven bullocks stand in grace,
Two rams and fourteen lambs, their presence embrace,
Meat offering and drink, with order unfold,
And a goat for sin offering, a story of old.

On the eighth day, a solemn assembly so grand,
No servile work, upon this sacred land,
Offer a bullock, a ram, seven lambs in delight,
Their meat offering and drink, a symphony's flight.

A goat for sin offering, beside the continuous flame,
With meat offering and drink, bearing a holy name,
These set feasts, your vows, offerings free,
Burnt, meat, drink, peace offerings, as I decree.

Moses shared these words, each detail and lore,
According to the Lord's command, the truth they store.

THE VALIDITY OF VOWS

Moses spoke to the heads of the tribes with care,
Regarding vows and oaths, a truth to share,
The command of the Lord, he did impart,
Guidelines for vows that touch the heart.

When a man vows or binds his soul with a chain,
He must uphold his word, not break it in vain,
Every promise and vow that his lips declare,
He shall fulfill, the Lord's truth to bear.

If a woman, too, makes a vow to God's name,
And binds herself with a bond, her soul aflame,
In her father's house, when she's young and fair,
Her vows shall stand, if he lets them bear.

But if her father objects, her vows to deny,
None of her promises shall reach the sky,
The Lord will forgive, her vows He'll erase,
If her father nullifies with a solemn grace.

And if a married woman's vow takes flight,
Her husband's silence means it's right,
But if he disapproves, on that very day,
Her vow shall fade, the Lord's word obey.

The vows of a widow, a divorced heart,
Shall stand, no man can set them apart,
Yet within a husband's house, a vow may rise,
And if he's silent, it will reach the skies.

But if her husband annuls them in his might,
Her vow and bond shall be made light,
The Lord will forgive, the burden He'll release,
For he made them void, and gave her peace.

A vow to afflict one's soul, a binding oath,
A husband may establish, or put them both,
If he remains silent, they shall remain,
Confirmed by his quiet, free from stain.

If later, he cancels them in their bloom,
He shall bear her iniquity, her due gloom,
These are the statutes, the Lord's command,
Guiding vows and oaths in the land.

Between a man and his wife, this truth does stand,
Between father and daughter, hand in hand,
When she's young and dwelling in her father's care,
These rules for vows, they both must share.

FLAMES OF RETRIBUTION

The Lord spoke to Moses and gave command,
To avenge the Israelites, to take a stand,
Against the Midianites, they must fight,
To set things straight and make things right.

Moses spoke to the people, firm and clear,
"Arm yourselves for battle, have no fear,
Avenge the Lord against Midian's might,
For they caused transgression, brought blight."

A thousand from each tribe, they prepared,
Twelve thousand armed, none were spared,
Phinehas, the priest, with holy might,
Took holy instruments and trumpets of light.

They fought against Midian, as God decreed,
They slew all the males, to succeed,
The kings of Midian they defeated,
Balaam too, his fate was completed.

Women and children were taken in stride,
Their livestock and goods, by the Israelites' side,
The cities they burned, the castles so grand,
The spoils of victory in their hand.

Moses and Eleazar, priests so true,
Met them outside the camp, as they were due,
Moses was angered, officers he did chide,
For sparing the women, he couldn't abide.

These were the ones who led astray,
Israel to sin, led them astray,
In the matter of Peor, they brought shame,
A plague upon Israel, a painful claim.

"Kill every male child," Moses did decree,
And every woman who knew man intimately,
But spare the virgin women pure,
For they had not known such a lure.

After battle, they were to be cleansed,
On the third and seventh days, offense dispensed,
All that had touched death, or suffered the same,
Were purified, free from blame.

Gold, silver, and metals strong,
Were to be purified, made right and long,
Passed through the fire and washed anew,
Cleansed and consecrated, the law to pursue.

Then the Lord spoke to Moses again,
To count the spoils, both beast and men,
Divide the plunder, and levy a fee,
A tribute to God, from the victory.

From the men of war, one in five hundred, to take,
From cattle and livestock, a portion to make,
Give it to Eleazar, the priest of grace,
A heave offering, a holy embrace.

And from Israel's share, a portion to give,
One in fifty, as long as they live,
To the Levites who served, the tabernacle's call,
A portion of the bounty, shared by all.

Moses and Eleazar, obeyed the divine,
Divided the spoils as the Lord's design,
The officers, captains, brought their tribute pure,
Gold and jewels, a sacred cure.

This gold was for offerings, a memorial kept,
In the tabernacle of God, it was well kept,
A reminder for Israel, of victory's song,
To the Lord, they gave tribute, righting the wrong.

BEYOND THE RIVER

The tribes of Reuben and Gad, so vast,
Had a multitude of cattle unsurpassed,
Seeing Jazer and Gilead's fertile ground,
A place for their cattle, they had found.

They came to Moses and the priest in might,
To princes of the congregation's light,
They listed cities, land in their view,
Where they could settle, their request they drew.

Ataroth, Dibon, Jazer, and more,
The land they'd conquered in days of yore,
They asked that this land, so rich and wide,
Be given to them as their chosen side.

"Grant us this land," they said to Moses strong,
"And let us stay here, it's where we belong,
We have much cattle, a multitude,
Please let us dwell here, with gratitude."

Moses questioned them with a heart concerned,
"Will you sit here while your brethren are burned,
By battles fierce, on the other side,
Will you not fight, with them abide?"

He reminded them of their fathers past,
Who faltered at Kadesh, their courage didn't last,
They discouraged Israel from the Promised Land,
And God's anger upon them did land.

Only Joshua and Caleb stood the test,
Following God with unwavering zest,
The rest perished in the desert's strife,
Forty years of wandering, a painful life.

Moses warned them of the consequences dire,
Their actions might kindle the Lord's fire,
If they turned from Him, they'd share the blame,
And all of Israel could be brought to shame.

They proposed a compromise, a pact so bold,
"We'll build our cities, our sheepfolds to hold,
We'll fight for Israel, to their place we'll guide,
And in fortified cities, our families will bide."

Moses agreed, if they fought with might,
Crossing Jordan and waging the fight,
When the land was subdued, they could return,
And their possession in Gilead, they'd earn.

But if they failed to fulfill this task,
Their sin would find them, no mask,
Build your cities and folds for your sheep,
Do as you've promised, your word to keep.

Gad and Reuben agreed to obey,
"We'll fight for Israel, come what may,
We'll cross the Jordan, armed and true,
To the land of Canaan, we'll see it through."

Moses then gave orders to leaders wise,
Eleazar and Joshua, without disguise,
The children of Gad and Reuben, so brave,
Could possess Gilead, the land they'd save.

So the tribes settled with their chosen land,
Gad built cities, Reuben took a stand,
The kingdom of Sihon, the land they claimed,
And cities they built, with new names acclaimed.

Machir of Manasseh took Gilead's reign,
Jair took small towns, a kingdom to maintain,
Nobah renamed Kenath, his banner unfurled,
A testament to their place in the world.

GILEAD'S ALLURE

These are the journeys the Israelites made,
From Egypt's land, with armies arrayed,
Guided by Moses and Aaron's care,
Their path and progress, a tale to share.

As commanded by the Lord above,
Moses wrote their travels with great love,
From Rameses they did depart,
With Passover's memory in their heart.

On the morrow after the feast so grand,
They left Egypt's shores, a chosen band,
Their high hand before Egyptians shown,
God's mighty power to be known.

The firstborn of Egypt, God had slain,
Their gods brought low, none could remain,
From Rameses to Succoth they went,
Their journey's tale, to history sent.

To Etham's edge, the next they came,
Turning to Pihahiroth's famed name,
By Migdol they pitched their tent,
Through parted seas, God's hand was sent.

Three days they wandered, the desert's grace,
From Marah's well to Elim's space,
With fountains pure and palm trees fair,
In Elim's shade, they rested there.

By the Red Sea, their camp was set,
In Sin's wilderness, they met,
Through journeys long, their faith was tried,
By God's hand, they would abide.

From Sin's wilds to Dophkah they went,
To Alush's camp, their steps were bent,
Rephidim next, where no water flowed,
God's miracle by Moses showed.

Through Sinai's wilderness they strayed,
In Kibrothhattaavah, their tents were laid,
To Hazeroth, their journey led,
Then on to Rithmah's camp they sped.

Rimmonparez and Libnah's space,
Rissah, Kehelathah, they embraced,
To mount Shapher, their feet did tread,
And Haradah's camp, they called their bed.

Makheloth, Tahath, and Tarah they passed,
Pitching their tents, the journey vast,
From Mithcah to Hashmonah's claim,
Then to Moseroth, their journey's aim.

Benejaakan and Horhagidgad's sight,
Jotbathah's camp, where they spent the night,
Ebronah, Eziongaber, on they went,
To Kadesh's land, their steps were bent.

Mount Hor's edge, where Aaron lay,
Commanded by God, he passed away,
A hundred and twenty-three years old,
His life's story beautifully told.

King Arad the Canaanite heard their name,
As Israel's children their journey came,
Zalmonah, Punon, Oboth they reached,
To Ijeabarim's border, their steps beseeched.

Dibongad, Almondiblathaim next in line,
To mountains of Abarim, a path divine,
Plains of Moab, by Jordan's shore,
Near Jericho's walls, their journey's core.

By Jordan's banks, their tents unfurled,
From Bethjesimoth to Abelshittim, a world,
There, the Lord to Moses did impart,
Commands for their future, from the heart.

"Drive out inhabitants, idols destroy,
High places topple, their false gods deploy,
Dispossess the land, make it your own,
Inheritance by lot, for each tribe shown.

The more shall receive a greater share,
The fewer, less, it's only fair,
In the place where your lot shall fall,
Shall be your inheritance, one and all.

But if you let inhabitants remain,
They'll be thorns and pricks, causing you pain,
Their ways will vex you, in your dwelling place,
Just as I intended, they'll mar your grace."

So the journeys of Israel, a tale so grand,
Guided by God's almighty hand,
Through trials and tests, they moved ahead,
Inheritors of a land, as God had said.

DESERT OF SIN

The Lord spoke to Moses, his command was clear,
In Canaan's land, when you draw near,
This land, your inheritance, it shall be,
With its borders and coasts, for all to see.

Your southern edge, from Zin's desert so wide,
By Edom's coast, where the salt sea's tide,
Shall mark your south border, by Akrabbim's way,
To Kadeshbarnea, where you shall stay.

To Hazaraddar and Azmon's light,
Your border shall pass, clear and bright,
Then on to the river of Egypt's end,
At the sea's shore, your bounds extend.

On the western side, the great sea wide,
Shall be your border, where waters abide,
From the mount Hor, northward you'll go,
To Hamath's entrance, the border shall show.

From Zedad, to Ziphron's path you'll trace,
To Hazarenan, your border's embrace,
The eastern boundary, from Hazarenan's site,
Shall reach to Shepham, where it takes its flight.

From Shepham down to Riblah's side,
East of Ain, where waters bide,
Your border shall descend, toward the sea,
Chinnereth's shore, where the waters be.

Down to Jordan's banks, the border flows,
Where the salt sea's end, its journey shows,
This is the land, its coasts surround,
The inheritance that you have found.

Moses commanded with words so clear,
To Israel's children, far and near,
This land, by lot, you shall obtain,
Nine tribes and a half, their share to gain.

Reuben, Gad, and Manasseh, they took,
Their inheritance, by the Lord's own book,
East of Jordan's flow, they claimed their stake,
Near Jericho's walls, their place to make.

Then Moses received a divine decree,
The names of those who would oversee,
The land's division, as the Lord planned,
By Eleazar and Joshua's hand.

From each tribe, a prince shall arise,
To divide the land, 'neath open skies,
Caleb of Judah, with faith so bold,
Shemuel of Simeon, his story told.

Elidad of Benjamin, he did stand,
As prince of his tribe, a leader grand,
Bukki of Dan, his duty to fulfill,
And others named, each with a skill.

Hanniel of Manasseh, tribe of the west,
Kemuel of Ephraim, their lot possessed,
Elizaphan of Zebulun, he did abide,
As prince of his tribe, by the Lord's side.

Paltiel of Issachar, Asher's Ahihud,
Pedahel of Naphtali, their names so good,
These are the leaders, as the Lord decreed,
To divide the land, to meet every need.

So the children of Israel, in Canaan's domain,
Received their inheritance, without any stain,
Divided by leaders, chosen and just,
A land of promise, in God they trust.

INHERITANCE MAPPING

In the plains of Moab by Jordan's flow,
The Lord to Moses did command and show,
To give the Levites cities for their space,
And suburbs too, for their cattle's grace.

Cities for dwelling, the Levites would gain,
Suburbs for goods, and beasts' domain,
The suburbs round, a thousand shall they be,
Beyond the city, as the Lord set free.

Two thousand cubits, on each side they'll see,
East, south, west, and north, the boundary be,
The city within, midst of suburbs wide,
A place of dwelling, where Levites reside.

Of these, six cities shall be sanctified,
As refuge for those who'd killed unawares,
From the avenger's hand, they shall not die,
Till judged they stand before the congregation's stares.

Of iron, or stone, or hand weapon of wood,
If death is caused, by hatred or by hood,
The murderer shall die, the avenger's hand,
Shall take his life, as justice commands.

If without enmity, a thrust is made,
Or cast by chance, without plans laid,
The congregation shall decide the fate,
Between the slayer and revenger's weight.

If guilty deemed, to the city of refuge he'll go,
Till high priest's death, his dwelling so,
But if he leaves, and avenger takes his breath,
Outside the refuge's bounds, beyond its width,

The avenger's guilt shall not be found,
For high priest's death must mark this ground,
Until then, the slayer's stay secure,
In his possession, he shall endure.

Throughout the generations, this law will stand,
In every dwelling, throughout the land,
No satisfaction for murder, no compromise,
Only death shall answer such a crime.

Defile not the land with shed blood's stain,
For only by blood, it can be made clean,
So keep the statutes, do as God decreed,
For He, the Lord, among His people, takes heed.

WOMEN'S RIGHT TO INHERIT

The fathers of Gilead's kin, they came to speak,
Before Moses and the chiefs, with concerns unique,
They said, "The Lord has spoken to our lord so true,
To grant inheritance by lot, as He would construe.

Zelophehad's daughters, they should inherit land,
And if wed to men from other tribes, we understand,
Their inheritance will shift, be taken away,
To the tribe of their husbands, it will sway.

Yet, in the year of Jubilee, it will return,
To the tribe of their father, we discern,
Moses, you have heard, this matter now so clear,
The tribe of Joseph's sons, their request we revere."

And Moses heeded this divine command,
The daughters of Zelophehad were to stand,
Free to choose their husbands from their kin,
Within their father's tribe, their new lives would begin.

Inheritance wouldn't shift from tribe to tribe,
Each held their own, as their lives did prescribe,
Mahlah, Tirzah, Hoglah, Milcah, and Noah too,
Married their cousins, as the commandment they knew.

They wed within the tribe of Manasseh's fame,
Inheritance intact, in their family's name,
These are the commands and judgments divine,
Given by the Lord through Moses' line.

In the plains of Moab, by Jordan's shore,
Near Jericho's walls, this decree He bore,
The children of Israel, His word did they keep,
As in their inheritance, their faith ran deep.

FACING GIANTS

Moses spoke to Israel, by Jordan's shore,
Where wilderness and hills did blend and soar.
Overlooking the Red Sea, they stood as one,
Between Paran, Laban, Tophel, and Hazeroth's sun.

Eleven days' journey from Horeb's peak so grand,
To Kadeshbarnea's realm, where destiny's hand,
In the fortieth year, eleventh month's embrace,
Moses shared God's word, their path to trace.

He recounted triumphs, Sihon and Og's fall,
Amorite kings defeated, their power enthralled.
On this Moab land, on Jordan's verge so wide,
Moses began to proclaim, the law as their guide.

"Long enough you've stayed," he declared with might,
"Turn, journey ahead, towards lands yet in sight.
To Amorite heights, Canaan's divine plan,
From sea to Euphrates, at God's command.

The promised land awaits, by ancient decree,
To Abraham, Isaac, and Jacob, God's legacy.
Wise leaders and judges I've charged for your way,
To guide tribes and thousands, through night and day.

Fair judges commanded, impartial and just,
Decide without favor, in God we all trust.
Show no partiality, whether great or small,
For God's justice is perfect, embracing all.

Remember the journey, through wilderness vast,
From Horeb to Kadesh, trials unsurpassed.
God led with a cloud by day, fire by night,
Like a father with a child, His guiding light.

Yet fear gripped your hearts, doubts took their hold,
In tents you murmured, your faith was untold.
You accused God of hate, in your uncertain flight,
Afraid of Amorite power, of losing the fight.

"Fear not," I proclaimed, "God's hand guides your way,
As in Egypt's days, He'll lead come what may.
Through the wilderness wild, His presence was near,
As a father carries his child, dispelling all fear.

But your lack of faith, your doubts did persist,
Despite signs and guidance, God's care you'd resist.
A cloud led by day, fire by night's gleam,
Through dark and through light, His presence did beam.

Your words roused God's anger, His might was unveiled,
This wicked generation, His favor curtailed.
Except for Caleb, whose faith never ceased,
For his wholehearted trust, God's promise released.

Joshua, too, shall inherit the prize,
Strengthen his heart, let your faith rise.
For the young and the small, the land they'll embrace,
God's call they'll fulfill, His blessings they'll trace.

But you, turn away, from this fate's cruel hand,
Through the Red Sea's gate, to the wilderness sand.
You confessed your sin, ready to strive,
But God's presence withdrew, His guidance alive.

Amorites pursued, like bees they did swarm,
Chasing through Seir, in fury and storm.
To Hormah they pressed, in relentless array,
Yet your cries went unanswered, in Kadesh you'd stay.

For days you remained, in a sorrowful place,
Facing the consequences, God's path to embrace.

UTTER DESTRUCTION

Through the wilderness we charted our course,
Beside the Red Sea, guided by divine force,
Around Mount Seir, our path took shape,
God's guidance our anchor, no landscape to escape.

With a command, the Lord spoke to me,
"Circles complete, it's time to break free,
Turn northward now, my word to embrace,
Pass Esau's realm with caution in place."

"No provocation," He said, "Fears remain low,
Their land's not your gift, no tears need you show,
Seir's their home, their legacy and claim,
Esau's possession, respected by name."

Trade with Esau's kin, their blessings unveiled,
Silver and gold, for provisions availed,
Forty years past, God by our side,
Through wilderness vast, our needs supplied.

As with Moabites and Amorites' land,
Esau's success played God's written hand,
Cross Arnon River, Sihon's realm to confront,
Topple his power, his dominion affront.

God stirred fear 'mongst nations around,
Our renown echoed, trembling sound,
Messengers to Sihon's throne conveyed,
Peaceful words, no war's blade displayed.

"We seek passage, strife we shun,
With life's price, food and water won,
As Moabites and Esau's kin before,
Onward we journey, God's sunlight we adore."

Yet Sihon stood firm, heart sealed in ice,
Stubborn, obstinate, defying God's advice,
Denied our plea, clung to his domain,
God's purpose through his resistance plain.

"The land is yours," God's voice did ring,
"Claim Sihon's domain, as destiny's king,
Meet him at Jahaz, battle's fierce dance,
By God's hand, victory's chance."

Jahaz witnessed Sihon's desperate stand,
With forces arrayed, across the land,
God bestowed triumph, His might unveiled,
Sihon and his kin defeated, hopes curtailed.

Cities fell to us, none could withstand,
Men, women, children, the conqueror's brand,
Spoils and cattle, ours to gain,
Cities' treasures too, our rightful terrain.

Arnon to Gilead, no city could stand,
God's design executed by our hand,
Triumphant over all, with God's aid,
Resistance crumbled, His power displayed.

Ammonites' realm we chose to forgo,
Jabbok River's domain, restraint to show,
Obeying God's call, boundaries heeding,
Following His path, faith never receding.

SPOILS AS PREY

Upon Bashan's path we turned our gaze,
Where Og, the king, in battle's blaze,
With all his people by his side,
Stood against us, fearless and pride.

But the Lord's voice whispered in my ear,
"Fear not, for victory is near.
Og and his lands I'll give to thee,
As I did Sihon's, so shall it be."

With God's might, we struck them down,
Og's power crumbled, his kingdom's crown.
Cities, sixty, we did claim,
Argob's region, bearing Og's name.

Fenced with walls, these cities stood,
Gates and bars like guardians good,
And in their midst, unwalled did gleam,
Towns many, like a hopeful dream.

We wiped them out, man, woman, child,
Innocence lost, lands turned wild.
Yet cattle and spoils for us to keep,
From the cities we conquered deep.

The lands of kings, beyond Jordan's shore,
From Arnon's river to Hermon's core,
We took from Amorite kings, twain,
As part of God's destined reign.

Hermon, named Sirion too,
By Sidon's voice and Amorite's view,
All the cities, plain and hill,
Gilead and Bashan, their souls fulfill.

Og, last of giants, stood alone,
His iron bedstead, a tale well-known,
Nine cubits long and four in breadth,
In Rabbath's halls, a tale he bequeathed.

Aroer by Arnon, half Gilead's might,
Cities there, a sacred sight,
Reuben and Gad their share did gain,
By river's edge, they'd remain.

Gilead's rest to Machir I gave,
An inheritance mighty and brave.
Reuben and Gad, by Arnon's shore,
Half the valley's stretch they bore.

The plains and Jordan, their edges traced,
Chinnereth's touch to the salt sea faced,
Under Ashdoth-pisgah's watchful stare,
The promised land lay, vast and rare.

My command to you, warriors bold,
With weapons true and spirits untold,
Cross with your kin, the battle true,
For God's land, He gives to you.

Yet wives and young, and cattle fair,
In cities dwell with tender care,
Until your brethren find their rest,
In lands beyond Jordan, they'll be blessed.

To Joshua, my charge was clear,
The Lord's wonders he'd soon revere,
Fear not, for God fights by your side,
To kingdoms unknown, you shall stride.

In prayer I knelt, my voice did rise,
Oh, Lord, reveal thy grand skies,
Thy works and might no equal know,
In heaven's heights and earth below.

Let me pass, see beyond the Jordan's rim,
That goodly mountain, majestic and dim,
But the Lord in anger turned His face,
My plea denied, His will in place.

To Pisgah's peak, I climbed alone,
Gazed west, north, south, east, all known,
Yet Jordan's waters I'd not cross,
Joshua's charge, his destined loss.

So we dwelt, by Bethpeor's side,
In the valley's calm, we did bide,
A journey's end, a tale untold,
As history's pages continued to unfold.

IDOLATRY'S TRAP

Hear, O Israel, my words of grace,
The laws, judgments, take your place,
To live and thrive, your land embrace,
As the Lord's gift, your rightful space.

Add not, subtract not, hold them true,
His commandments, old and new,
Keep them close, in all you do,
The Lord's path, let it guide you through.

Remember Baalpeor's dire fate,
Those who strayed met a bitter state,
Cleave to the Lord, don't hesitate,
In His embrace, you shall await.

Wisdom and understanding shall you gain,
A beacon to nations, their minds will train,
"Great is this people," they'll exclaim,
A wise, understanding, shining flame.

No nation boasts a God so near,
To answer prayers, to calm your fear,
With righteous laws, so pure and clear,
This law divine, hold it dear.

Watch yourself, lest memories fade,
From your heart, the truth evade,
Teach your kin, the legacy made,
From generation to generation's trade.

At Horeb's mount, in awe you stood,
Fire and clouds, a sight so good,
God's voice you heard, misunderstood,
No form, just His words, like firewood.

Covenant unveiled, commands so true,
Ten on stone, a guiding view,
Taught to you, now teach the crew,
In the land you'll conquer, anew.

No idols craft, no images bright,
Beasts, fowl, or stars of the night,
To these, don't bow in blind delight,
The Lord alone, your guiding light.

Lift not your eyes, heavenward gaze,
Sun, moon, stars in their cosmic maze,
Serve them not in misguided ways,
The Lord's command, forever stays.

From Egypt's forge, the Lord set you free,
A people of inheritance, a destiny,
Angered by me, this land I can't see,
But you shall thrive, and dwell in glee.

Take heed, lest the covenant you forget,
Graven images, God's path beset,
For He's a consuming fire, don't let
His wrath ignite, a danger met.

When days are long, in the land you stay,
Evil tempts, straying far astray,
Seek the Lord, in earnest pray,
With heart and soul, find His way.

In tribulation, when troubles swell,
Turn to the Lord, His voice compel,
A merciful God, who loves you well,
He won't forsake, as history will tell.

From days of old to the present view,
Search the world through and through,
Has such a wondrous thing e'er grew?
God's voice heard by me and you?

God's mighty hand, His outstretched arm,
From Egypt's grasp, He'd charm,
Nations driven away, to grant you farm,
Inherit their land, without alarm.

Know today, in heart and soul,
The Lord is God, above control,
Keep His statutes, reach your goal,
Long days upon this earth, you'll stroll.

Three cities stood, a haven near,
For those who fled in sudden fear,
No vengeance here, no danger here,
A place of refuge, safety clear.

These are the laws, the truths to bind,
Moses' testament, to all mankind,
On this side Jordan, you shall find,
In Sihon's land, where destinies intertwined.

Remember well the path you trod,
From Egypt's clasp, through deserts broad,
The land you claimed, with iron rod,
From Aroer's bank to Hermon's nod.

Eastward stretch, the Jordan's side,
To Pisgah's springs, where waters glide,
This law, a beacon, none can hide,
With love and grace, let it be your guide.

DESIRES FORBIDDEN

Gather 'round, O Israel, lend an ear,
Hear the statutes, judgments clear,
I speak them now, hold them dear,
Learn, obey, let no doubt appear.

In Horeb's realm, a covenant made,
With us alone, this bond displayed,
Our fathers knew not this crusade,
To us, this pact, God's grace conveyed.

The Lord met you, face to face,
From fiery mount, His words did grace,
I stood between, the sacred space,
Revealing His word, a wondrous trace.

"I am your God," His voice did say,
From Egypt's chains, He led the way,
None shall come before Me, don't sway,
Bow not to idols, nor their display.

No image carved, no likeness seen,
In heaven's realm, or earth's serene,
Bow not to them, nor worship keen,
For the Lord's name, keep it clean.

Remember the day, the sabbath's call,
Six days labor, tasks stand tall,
But the seventh day, let work's chain fall,
Rest for all, a sacred thrall.

Honoring father and mother, the creed,
Days prolonged, success guaranteed,
Thou shalt not kill, in this truth heed,
Adultery shun, and every ill deed.

Stealing, false witness, coveting naught,
These principles, by which to be taught,
Neighbor's wife, field, ox, all sought,
From ill desires, keep your thoughts.

God's words echoed from the fiery space,
Cloud, darkness, His mighty grace,
On stone tablets, His law we embrace,
Given to me, a sacred chase.

In darkness's midst, His voice we heard,
The mountain flamed, awe incurred,
Tribal heads, elders stirred,
God's glory seen, His voice assured.

"We've heard God's voice," the people said,
From midst of fire, His voice widespread,
Talking with man, a path widespread,
Why face this fire, risk life instead?

Such is the fear, the flames alight,
This fire's grandeur, consuming might,
For who survived, hearing this right?
God's voice, too vast for mortal sight.

Approach, hear God's voice unfold,
Speak to us, your words be told,
We'll heed His call, in His ways mold,
His teachings vast, His wisdom gold.

God heard their plea, their earnest plea,
Well spoken words, sincere decree,
O that hearts held fear, reverence be,
Commandments kept, for eternity.

Return to your tents, the order clear,
Stand with me now, hold words near,
I'll unveil laws, judgments dear,
In this promised land, without fear.

Observe, obey, don't turn aside,
To left or right, let truth abide,
Walk in His ways, no need to hide,
Life, blessings vast, forever to guide.

KEEP THEM CLOSE

These are the laws, the statutes profound,
The judgments too, where wisdom's found,
God's commands to teach, to spread around,
In the land you'll claim, on sacred ground.

Fear the Lord, with reverence hold,
His statutes, commandments, untold,
Passed through generations, young and old,
Prolong your days, blessings unfold.

O Israel, listen well, obey,
In this land of milk and honey's sway,
Increase, thrive, as God's word display,
Promised by fathers, bright as day.

Hear, O Israel, His voice embrace,
One Lord, our God, the guiding grace,
Love Him with heart, soul's sacred space,
With all your might, His path you trace.

Keep these words, in your heart engrain,
Teach your children, this truth maintain,
In your house, on journeys, in joy and pain,
Upon your hand, as frontlets, remain.

Write on your doorposts, gates so grand,
God's commands, a faithful brand,
For in the promised land you stand,
A covenant etched, forever to withstand.

When into the land, God guides your way,
Great cities rise, where you'll stay,
Houses and wells, blessings array,
Remember His hand, every single day.

Beware forgetting God's mighty hand,
From Egypt's land, He freed your band,
Fear, serve, with an oath withstand,
Bow not to idols, in any land.

He's a jealous God, so beware,
Anger kindled, a fate to bear,
Tempt Him not, His patience wear,
Observe His ways, show Him you care.

Keep His commandments, hold them true,
Do what's right, in His sight pursue,
Inherit the land, as He vowed to you,
Enemies vanquished, the promise comes through.

When your children ask, in days to unfold,
About God's statutes, stories of old,
Share the tale, of Egypt's hold,
His mighty hand, signs untold.

From bondage brought, by wondrous might,
Signs, wonders, in day and night,
From Egypt's grasp, you took your flight,
To claim a land, in God's pure light.

These statutes, for our good, God's decree,
Preserving us, His wisdom free,
Righteousness found in obedience, you see,
In His commands, our path shall be.

FORBIDDEN ALLIANCES

As you enter the land you're bound to gain,
Nations expelled, in victory's reign,
Hittites, Girgashites, their names plain,
Seven mighty foes, you shall detain.

God shall deliver them, don't hold back,
Smite and destroy them on their track,
No covenant made, no mercy's lack,
Their altars razed, no offerings stack.

Marriage bonds with them shall not be,
For they'll lead your son to idolatry,
Turn him from Me, their gods he'll see,
My anger fierce, destruction decree.

Break their altars, idols deface,
Groves and images erase,
Into the fire, let them efface,
All their idols, no trace to trace.

A holy people, set apart,
Chosen by God, a sacred heart,
Not for your numbers, a special part,
His love and promise, never depart.

Out of Egypt's grip, with a mighty hand,
Redeemed from Pharaoh's cruel land,
God's oath fulfilled, His faithful stand,
Led by His love, a chosen band.

Know this, the Lord is true and just,
Covenant and mercy, in Him we trust,
With love He blesses, in Him we adjust,
Generations to come, in Him we entrust.

He repays those who hate His name,
To their face, their deeds aflame,
For those who love, His blessings claim,
Keep His commands, His eternal fame.

Observe His statutes, judgments, true,
Do them faithfully, as He'd construe,
For if you obey, blessings accrue,
His covenant and mercy, forever in view.

Love, blessings, increase shall unfold,
Abundant fruit, blessings untold,
Sickness banished, His grace to hold,
A blessed people, in His stronghold.

No barrenness, be it man or beast,
God's blessings shall never cease,
No plagues of Egypt, but joy released,
On those who follow, His covenant's feast.

The nations you conquer, don't spare,
No pity shown, no gods to share,
Don't be ensnared, their gods beware,
Serve them not, for your souls take care.

If their numbers make you quail,
Remember God's power, without fail,
How Pharaoh's might and Egypt's jail,
God's miracles crushed their scale.

The wonders you saw, the temptations grand,
His mighty hand, like a stretched-out hand,
He'll do the same for every land,
Before whom you tremble, take your stand.

God will send the hornet's sting,
Among the foes, confusion bring,
Till they're destroyed, to His wrath cling,
No fear in your heart, let courage spring.

For the Lord your God is by your side,
Mighty and awesome, in Him confide,
He'll drive away the foes worldwide,
But not all at once, let them subside.

Little by little, their strength will wane,
Lest beasts of the field, on you they rain,
Deliver them to you, their fate ordained,
Destroy their kings, their name disdain.

Burn their idols with fire's might,
Silver and gold, shun from sight,
Don't take for yourself, in their light,
For they're abominations, hidden or bright.

Bring not abominations, cursed they be,
Into your house, let none of them flee,
Detest and abhor them, let it decree,
For cursed they are, a curse they'll decree.

WALK IN HIS WAYS

Observe these commands that I bestow,
To live, multiply, and possess the land we'll know,
Remember the path the Lord did show,
In the wilderness, His lessons we'd undergo.

For forty years, He led us through,
To humble and test, to make us true,
He allowed hunger, manna He'd strew,
To teach, by His word, we live, not by bread's hue.

No aging raiment, nor swollen feet,
For forty years, His care complete,
Like a father who chastens, our path to meet,
God's commandments obey, His ways to greet.

He leads us to a land of grace,
With brooks and fountains, a fertile place,
Wheat, barley, vines, a fruitful embrace,
Olives, honey, blessings to trace.

A land with abundance, no scarcity to find,
Stones of iron, brass to unbind,
When fullness and blessing in life are twined,
Remember the Lord, in thanks be aligned.

Beware, lest pride in your heart takes root,
Commandments, judgments, statutes to dispute,
In goodly houses, comfort to suit,
Lest God's blessings, His grace, you dilute.

As herds, flocks, silver, and gold increase,
Your heart's pride could bring a decrease,
Forget not God's hand, His mercies' lease,
From Egypt's bondage, His mighty release.

Through wilderness vast, with trials faced,
Fiery serpents and drought's harsh taste,
He gave us water, from flint rock's chaste,
Manna, to humble, His goodness embraced.

Never think, "My power, my hand has gained,
This wealth and success," let it not be explained,
Remember God's role, His covenant maintained,
He gives power for wealth, His promise sustained.

But if you forsake Him, other gods embrace,
Serve and worship them, in their embrace,
A testimony against you, judgment's trace,
Perish you shall, like nations misplaced.

As nations before us faced destruction's rod,
You too shall perish, if you disregard,
Obedience to God's voice, your path marred,
Choose the Lord's way, your life safeguarded.

THE GOLDEN CALF INCIDENT

Listen, O Israel, as you cross the Jordan today,
To possess lands and cities in your way,
Nations tall and strong, greater than you,
Anakims' children, formidable and true.

Know this day, the Lord goes before you,
A consuming fire, His power true,
He'll bring them down, and cast them out,
Swiftly destroyed, there's no room for doubt.

But in your heart, don't boast of your might,
Or claim that your righteousness brought this sight,
Not for your goodness, but their wicked ways,
The Lord drives them out, fulfilling His gaze.

Understand, this land is not yours by right,
But for the promise, to Abraham's line so bright,
For you are stubborn, a stiffnecked race,
Rebellious in heart, and lost in grace.

Remember the wilderness, how you provoked,
God's wrath and anger, His patience revoked,
At Horeb, you angered Him, rebellion you chose,
In His sight, your disobedience arose.

When to the mountain, I ascended high,
To receive the covenant, written by,
Upon stone tablets, with God's own hand,
To guide you, to lead you, to help you stand.

But in that time, you turned away,
Quickly straying, led your hearts astray,
A molten calf you did create,
God's commandments, you did forsake.

I cast the tablets, broken they lay,
Before your eyes, a display,
Of your sin and rebellion, against the Lord,
A solemn reminder of His accord.

For forty days and nights, I pleaded,
Fasted and prayed, my voice was needed,
To save you from God's burning ire,
From His anger's consuming fire.

Fearful, I stood, before His might,
Afraid of His wrath, the impending fight,
But the Lord listened, He did relent,
In mercy, He spared, His judgment He bent.

Aaron too faced God's fierce wrath,
Angry with him, on a destructive path,
I interceded for his fate,
And God's anger did abate.

I took your sin, the molten calf's form,
Burned it, crushed it, destroyed its norm,
Into the brook, the dust did flee,
A symbol of sin, forever to be.

At Taberah, Massah, and Kibrothhattaavah,
You provoked God's anger, a dangerous lava,
Even at Kadeshbarnea, you doubted His call,
Rebellion persisted, in defiance you'd fall.

From the day I knew you, rebellious you've been,
Forty days and nights, I pled for your sin,
I begged God, "Don't destroy, don't erase,
This people redeemed, by Your powerful grace."

Remember Abraham, Isaac, and Jacob, Your own,
Look past our stubbornness, the seeds of sin sown,
Don't let the world say, "God's power is weak,
He led them to perish, the future looks bleak."

These people are Yours, Your inheritance, Your hand,
Brought out of Egypt, through desert sand,
By Your mighty power, Your outstretched arm,
Don't forsake us now, keep us from harm.

LOVING THE STRANGER

At that time, the Lord said to me,
"Hew two new stones, like the first, you see,
And ascend the mount, bring wood to make,
An ark for the tables, My word's sake.

So I hewed stone tables, like the first,
Carried them to the mount, my heart did burst,
The words of the Lord, I knew to write,
Upon those stones, shining pure and bright.

He wrote the commandments, as before,
Words of wisdom, truths to explore,
The ten commands, His sacred law,
Given once more, without a flaw.

Down I came from the mount on high,
With tablets in hand, beneath the sky,
Placed them within the ark of wood,
As God commanded, pure and good.

Israel journeyed on, a path anew,
From Beeroth to Mosera, a journey true,
Aaron passed, his son took his place,
Eleazar served with sacred grace.

From Gudgodah to Jotbath's land,
Rivers flowed, a watery strand,
The tribe of Levi, set apart,
To bear the ark, with faithful heart.

Levi had no portion, no land to claim,
God's inheritance, His holy name,
In the mount, I stayed once more,
Forty days, His mercy did pour.

Arise, said the Lord, journey forth,
Before the people, show your worth,
Possess the land, as promised of old,
A destiny awaiting, a story to be told.

So, Israel, hear what God desires,
To fear and love, as love requires,
Walk in His ways, with heart and soul,
Keep His commands, your life's true goal.

The heavens, and heavens of heavens, proclaim,
The Lord's domain, His majestic name,
He chose your fathers, His love did unfold,
Chose you above all, a story to be told.

Circumcise your hearts, be not stiff-necked,
In love, God's commands, accept and accept,
He is Lord of lords, God of gods supreme,
He judges justly, cares for the unseen.

Love the stranger, as He has done,
For you were strangers, under Egypt's sun,
Fear the Lord your God, cleave to His name,
Serve and honor Him, in His holy flame.

He is your praise, your God so great,
For wondrous deeds, don't hesitate,
Your fathers, a small and humble band,
Now you're countless, as stars in the sky's expanse.

CARE FOR THE LAND

Love the Lord thy God, keep His decree,
His laws, His judgments, His commands, hold thee,
Know this, O Israel, for your offspring new,
Not seen God's might, His chastisement true.

His mighty hand, His outstretched arm's embrace,
Miracles in Egypt, in that time and place,
Against the Egyptian army's might,
He drowned them in the Red Sea's night.

In the wilderness, His guidance clear,
His wonders shown to eyes that peer,
Dathan and Abiram, remember well,
Swallowed by earth, a solemn spell.

Your eyes have seen His acts so grand,
Upon this sacred, chosen land,
Keep His commands with all your might,
Be strong and enter, day and night.

Inherit a land, flowing with grace,
A land of hills, heaven's rain embrace,
The Lord's eyes upon it, always to see,
From year's start to end, eternally.

If you listen, love, and serve true,
Obey His words, and His will pursue,
He'll send rain in season, blessings unbound,
Abundance and growth, in fields all around.

Grass for your cattle, and food to eat,
Take heed, lest you falter, and God's path retreat,
Serve not other gods, be faithful and just,
Lest God's wrath descend, in Him put your trust.

Bind His words to heart and soul,
A sign on your hand, a goal to uphold,
Teach your children, night and day,
Write on doorposts, His words display.

Multiply your days as heaven's light,
Keep His commands, walk in His sight,
Obey His ways, cleave to His name,
Drive out nations, possess in His fame.

Every place you tread shall be yours,
From wilderness wild to distant shores,
Fear of you will be laid upon the land,
As God promised, under His command.

Blessings and curses before you stand,
Obedience leads to a promised land,
Mount Gerizim's height with blessings graced,
Mount Ebal, a curse, the path misplaced.

Beyond Jordan's flow, the journey calls,
To possess the land where God's grace falls,
Observe His statutes, judgments true,
Live by His word, let His light shine through.

THE SANCTITY OF BLOOD

In the land that God your fathers gave,
Observe these statutes all your days,
Destroy their altars, pillars too,
Burn their groves and images, so true.

Seek the place God's name shall dwell,
Offer sacrifices, all vows to tell,
Rejoice before Him, household and kin,
For God's blessings shall dwell therein.

Do not choose your own path or way,
Follow God's guidance, day by day,
For you have not reached the final rest,
Inheritance, safety, when you're truly blessed.

When you cross the Jordan's tide,
Inherit the land, safe and wide,
A place where God's name will reside,
Bring offerings there, His commands to abide.

Rejoice before the Lord your God,
Together with those on His holy sod,
Share blessings with Levite, maids and men,
For they have no part or land to obtain.

Do not offer burnt offerings everywhere,
Only where God's chosen place is fair,
Eat flesh as you desire, unclean and clean,
But do not consume blood, it's life unseen.

Within your gates, do not consume,
Tithe, firstlings, vows, in your own room,
Eat before the Lord in His chosen place,
Rejoice and bless, in His endless grace.

Do not forsake the Levite's need,
Support them well, do a righteous deed,
When borders expand and distance is far,
Satisfy your soul's longing, as a guiding star.

In God's chosen place, you shall partake,
As the roebuck and hart, unclean and clean,
But never consume the blood, the life's stream,
Pour it on earth, not in stomachs to be seen.

Keep these laws, observe them well,
For your children's future, their stories to tell,
When nations are driven out, and you succeed,
Beware their ways, God's path you shall heed.

Do not inquire, or follow their path,
Their abominations, God's righteous wrath,
For they burned their children in fire's embrace,
Trust not in these deeds, seek God's saving grace.

Observe all I command, never subtract or add,
God's word is complete, to follow, be glad,
In these statutes and judgments, forever be true,
That you may find favor, in all you pursue.

IDOL'S END

If a prophet or dreamer arises, you see,
Performing signs or wonders, that may be,
Yet they speak of other gods, unknown,
Tempting you to paths not of God's own.

Do not heed that prophet's voice,
Nor follow the dreams of their choice,
For God tests your love, devotion so true,
To see if you wholeheartedly follow through.

Follow the Lord your God, fear and obey,
Keep His commandments, in His ways stay,
Cling to Him, serve Him with heart and soul,
For this is your purpose, your ultimate goal.

Should a prophet or dreamer divert your way,
Leading to gods of astray,
Such a one shall not endure,
For death shall be the consequence, sure.

Such a one will seek to sway,
From God's path, to go astray,
But to Him, you must remain,
Their false words, you shall disdain.

Even if a brother or kin entices you so,
Secretly suggesting other gods to know,
Do not yield to their wrongful plea,
Nor show them mercy, let them be free.

Stone them with stones, let them die,
Their actions provoke God's righteous cry,
For turning from the God who redeemed,
A crime severe, not to be deemed.

Should a city follow abhorrent lore,
And turn to gods not known before,
Investigate, inquire, and be sure,
If the abomination is pure.

If truth is found in their wicked deed,
And the cursed path they blindly feed,
Then with the sword, their city's fate,
Utter destruction, their end awaits.

Burn the city, its spoils erase,
A heap of ruins, in its place,
Let nothing cursed remain in hand,
So God's anger may cease and stand.

Obey the Lord's voice, His commands obey,
In His righteous path, always stay,
For His mercy and blessings will flow,
As you follow Him, His ways to know.

CARING FOR THE NEEDY

As children of the Lord, hear these words,
Guidance for life, like melodious birds.
Do not cut yourselves or shave your hair,
In mourning for the dead, beware.

You're holy to God, a chosen race,
Peculiar people, His love embrace.
Do not consume what's abominable and unclean,
In your diet, follow what's right and pristine.

Eat the ox, sheep, and goats with delight,
Hart, roebuck, and others in your sight,
Those that chew the cud, and split hooves in two,
Are the ones that are clean and right for you.

But those that only chew or hooves divide,
Are unclean, from them, you must hide,
The swine too, it divides its hoof,
But it doesn't chew cud, that's the proof.

In the waters, eat those with fins and scales,
Others unclean, to them set your sails.
Clean birds you can enjoy, their flesh eat,
But eagles, vultures, avoid in your feat.

Creeping creatures flying, unclean they stand,
For food, they're not meant in your land.
Of clean fowls, you're free to dine,
But things that die by themselves decline.

Give such to the stranger, outside your gate,
Or sell to an alien, that is your fate.
Never seethe a kid within its mother's milk,
Such a practice God's law does bilk.

Tithing you must do, year after year,
The first-fruits of all, without fear.
Before the Lord, eat in His chosen place,
Fear Him and seek His glorious grace.

If distance prevents, turn tithe to coin,
Take it to the place God's chosen, to join.
Use the money for desires of your soul,
Oxen, sheep, wine, or whatever is your goal.

Rejoice before the Lord with heart and voice,
With your household and the Levite, rejoice.
Don't forsake the Levite, he has no share,
Extend your compassion and loving care.

After three years, another rule you'll heed,
Lay up the tithe, to those in need.
Strangers, fatherless, widows, and more,
Blessings of God, upon you they'll pour.

PERPETUAL GENEROSITY

Every seventh year, release shall take place,
For creditors' debts, a divine embrace.
Let go of the loans you've given, be kind,
As the Lord's release, let it unwind.

With a neighbor or brother, be lenient,
But from foreigners, debts are different.
When the land is rich, poverty rare,
Observe the commands with due care.

Listen to God's voice, keep His ways,
Blessings will follow all your days.
Lend to nations, rule over their land,
God's favor upon you, firm and grand.

If a poor brother seeks your hand,
Open wide your heart, let him withstand.
Lend to him with heart and hand,
For blessings from God on you will land.

Do not harden your heart, nor withhold,
For God's blessings He'll unfold.
When the poor cry out to the Lord above,
Your lack of giving will be seen as a sin, no love.

Give freely to your brethren in need,
For this act, God's blessings will proceed.
Poverty will persist within your land,
So lend a hand, follow His command.

If a Hebrew servant you've employed,
After six years, let him be joyed.
As he leaves, let him not go bare,
Furnish him well, show God's care.

Remember your days in Egyptian chains,
God's mercy and redemption that sustains.
If the servant loves his place, stays near,
Pierce his ear, a sign of service clear.

The bondman and maidservant, the same rule,
Through their ear, their service will school.
Releasing them, don't be distressed,
God's blessings will follow, you'll be blessed.

Sanctify firstlings, males of the flock,
With no work, God's law you unlock.
Yearly before the Lord, you'll partake,
In the chosen place, God's command to make.

Offer without blemish, that is right,
Not lame, blind, or with a faulty sight.
Both clean and unclean may partake alike,
Blood, don't eat it, on the ground, let it strike.

FORBIDDEN IMAGES

Observe the month of Abib with care,
For in that time, God's mercy rare.
The Passover sacrifice to Him you'll make,
In the chosen place His name to partake.

No leavened bread shall touch the feast,
Seven days of unleavened, to say the least.
Bread of affliction, to remember the night,
Egypt's escape, God's guiding light.

No leavened bread, no flesh remain,
Throughout the feast, this you must maintain.
Not within your gates shall Passover be,
But where God's name rests, let it be free.

At sunset's hour, the offering made,
Roast and eat where God's presence's laid.
Return to your tents as morning draws near,
Six days unleavened, the seventh revered.

Seven weeks shall you count, with care,
From harvest's beginning, with crops to share.
The Feast of Weeks, with a joyful hand,
A freewill offering, as God's blessings expand.

Rejoice before God, your sons and your kin,
Levites and strangers, all enter in.
Remember your past as a slave in the land,
Observe God's commandments, obey His demand.

The Feast of Tabernacles, seven days to keep,
When harvest is gathered and treasures reap.
Rejoice in the feast, all join the delight,
Levite and stranger, all in God's sight.

Appear three times yearly before God's throne,
In the place He's chosen, His presence shown.
Unleavened Bread, Weeks, Tabernacles, these three,
Appear not empty-handed, as blessings shall be.

Give as you're able, in God's blessed hand,
According to blessings, He's given the land.
Set judges and officers in every gate,
Impartial judgment, don't let it abate.

Do not pervert justice, no favor shown,
Gifts can blind eyes, let righteousness be known.
Seek fairness in all, let justice prevail,
Live in the land with integrity's trail.

No groves by God's altar, trees not near,
No images set up, no idols to revere.
Observe God's commands, His will to embrace,
For in His ways, you'll find true grace.

CHOOSING A BROTHER

Do not offer to the Lord your God,
Any blemished cattle or sheep flawed.
Such offerings are an abomination,
In His presence, a grievous violation.

If a man or woman, in your midst,
Has transgressed God's covenant, resist.
Serving other gods, the heavenly host,
Stone them to death, such abominable boasts.

Two or three witnesses, their words align,
For a person worthy of death's design.
Their hands shall cast the first stones,
To cleanse the land from these wicked tones.

When disputes arise too complex to weigh,
To the chosen place, to the judges, obey.
The Levitical priests, the appointed judge,
Will offer guidance, wisdom they fudge.

According to their judgment, you shall act,
Their decision, you must not retract.
Follow their teaching, left or right,
Punish the presumptuous with righteous might.

When a king you set upon the throne,
A brother from your midst, not unknown.
He shall not amass horses from the land,
Nor lead the people back to Egypt's sand.

Wives and riches he shall not accumulate,
Lest his heart from God deviate.
A copy of the law he shall write,
Read it daily, day and night.

He shall learn to fear the Lord's name,
His commandments and statutes, the same.
Let his heart not be lifted in pride,
Keep God's ways, never to slide.

In his kingdom, he shall prolong his stay,
With his children, the righteous way.
Obey the law, with God's might,
To ensure his rule remains bright.

SEEKING TRUTH

The priests of Levi, no inheritance claim,
Their portion is the Lord's sacred flame.
Shoulder, cheeks, and maw, offerings of fire,
First fruits and fleece, their rightful desire.

Chosen to minister in God's holy name,
Levites stand before Him, a sacred aim.
If a Levite from afar desires to serve,
In the chosen place, his duty observe.

Abominations of nations don't partake,
Their ways and practices, forsake.
No child through fire, no divination's art,
No observer of times or enchanter's part.

No witch, charmer, consulter with the dead,
Such practices are abhorred, God has said.
Be perfect with the Lord your God in all,
Reject these deeds, stand firm, heed the call.

A Prophet like Moses, God will raise,
From your brethren, to lead and amaze.
Listen to His words, obey His voice,
For in Him, God's guidance and choice.

As in Horeb's assembly, the voice they feared,
God's response was that they rightly steered.
A Prophet like Moses He will send,
With His words, His commands to tend.

If a prophet speaks what God hasn't conveyed,
Or in other gods' name, plans are laid,
Death shall befall the presumptuous claim,
For speaking falsehoods in God's name is shame.

When a prophet's words don't come true,
The Lord's not spoken, be assured, it's not true.
Fear not such a prophet who falsely claims,
For God's truth prevails, dispelling falsehood's flames.

DETER EVIL

When lands of nations the Lord bestows,
In their cities and homes, you'll repose.
Three cities set apart with care,
For refuge, to flee when in despair.

Prepare the way, divide the land,
For those who need a saving hand.
A slayer, unintentional, may find,
In these cities, protection and peace of mind.

A man in the woods, his axe swings,
But a deathly blow, an accident brings.
To the city of refuge, he shall flee,
From the avenger, to be set free.

If hatred is absent, and death's blow falls,
The avenger pursues, as vengeance calls.
Three cities ensure, as the land expands,
Innocent blood shed not upon your hands.

But if hatred breeds a deadly plot,
And a man his neighbor's life has sought,
He shall be delivered to avenger's might,
Justice shall reign in the clear daylight.

No pity to show, guilt must be clear,
Innocent blood's stain you must not bear.
No landmarks shifted, a boundary's grace,
Respect for others' rights we embrace.

With one witness, accusations won't stand,
Two or three mouths, truth's pillars so grand.
A false witness, if falsehoods be spun,
Shall face the judgment before everyone.

Judges inquire, false witness to find,
Justice prevails, for lies we're maligned.
As he planned against his brother with deceit,
Likewise shall his punishment be complete.

Fear shall spread as justice is done,
Evil retreats, truth's battle is won.
No pity to show, life must pay for life,
Justice prevails, dispelling all strife.

Eye for eye, tooth for tooth, we find,
Equity in punishment, justice designed.
In these laws and rules, let righteousness thrive,
In the land of promise, let justice arrive.

OBLITERATING NATIONS

When facing foes with horses and might,
Fear not, for God's with you in the fight.
From Egypt's land, He brought you forth,
With His strength, your enemies will be north.

Approaching battle, the priest shall say,
"Fear not, for God's with you today.
Let not your hearts tremble or fear,
For God fights for you, His presence near."

Officers speak of duties clear,
For those with house, vineyard, or dear.
If you've just built, or your fields you've sown,
Return to them, they're yours to own.

For the fearful heart, let them depart,
Lest they weaken each comrade's heart.
When officers' words have been declared,
Captains of armies will be prepared.

To a city you march, make peace your plea,
If they respond, let them serve thee.
But if war is their chosen path,
Besiege the city in righteous wrath.

When victory comes to your hand,
The males by the sword's edge shall stand.
Yet women, children, cattle, and spoil,
Shall be yours as fruits of the toil.

In distant lands, show mercy's grace,
But these nearby, no trace to trace.
Hittites, Amorites, Canaanites too,
Perizzites, Hivites, Jebusites through.

Destroy them all, God's command obey,
Lest they lead you in abominable way.
But trees of the land, spare from the fight,
For man's life in them, take no unjust right.

Trees for food, let them stand tall,
The rest, in war, let their branches fall.
Build bulwarks strong, the city to subdue,
Until victory's yours, and peace breaks through.

CAPTIVE WIVES

If a slain man is found in the land,
And the killer's unknown, no one's hand,
Elders and judges shall come and trace,
Cities round about the death's grim space.

The nearest city, elders shall go,
Taking an unworn heifer to show,
Not yoked, not used, a sign to be,
In a valley rough, they shall set it free.

The priests, God's chosen, shall then appear,
To bless and judge, to make truth clear.
By their word, disputes shall be resolved,
Controversies settled, problems solved.

The elders shall wash their hands with care,
Over the heifer's bloodied neck laid bare.
They'll declare, "We're free from guilt and stain,
This blood is not on our hands, we proclaim.

Be merciful, Lord, to Israel's race,
Lay not innocent blood to their trace.
This act forgives, from blood guilt they're free,
Doing what's right in the sight of Thee.

When at war with foes, God's hand at play,
And captives you take on that day,
If a woman fair in captives you see,
Desiring her as your wife to be,

Bring her to your home, she shall mourn,
Cut her hair, her captive's clothes be torn.
Let her grieve her kin, a month to recall,
Then you shall enter, as husband, not thrall.

If your delight fades, let her be free,
Not for silver's gain, no commodity.
You've humbled her, let her find her way,
No ownership, no price to pay.

Two wives, one beloved, one not so,
Children borne by both, they grow.
But the firstborn's rights must be clear,
Even if mother's heart is dear.

If a son is stubborn, rebellious, untrue,
Defying both mother and father's view,
They shall bring him to elders and gate,
Declare his defiance, his twisted state.

The men of the city shall cast the stones,
Till his life ends, his rebellion dethrones.
So evil departs, as all will see,
Israel's lesson: respect and fear set free.

If a man is hanged, accursed of God,
Upon a tree, 'neath heaven's nod,
The body must not defile the land,
Bury him promptly by God's command.

LIFTING EACH OTHER UP

If your brother's ox or sheep go astray,
Don't hide yourself, don't turn away.
Bring them back, restore what's lost,
To your brother's possession, at any cost.

If he's not near, or you know not who,
Bring it home, guard it well, it's true.
Hold it till he seeks it out,
Return it to him, remove all doubt.

Likewise, do for his ass and his clothes,
With lost things, be fair, as righteousness shows.
Don't ignore when they stumble down,
Help them up, don't let them frown.

A woman shall not wear a man's attire,
Nor a man don what women require.
For all who break this sacred line,
An abomination, the Lord doth define.

If a bird's nest upon your path is found,
With eggs or young, upon the ground,
Take the young ones, let the dam be,
That you may live long, God's decree.

When you build a house, roof a battlement make,
Lest one fall and his life you take.
Mix not seeds in your vineyard's space,
Lest your harvest's purity you deface.

Don't yoke an ox and an ass as one,
Different strengths, not a team well done.
Garments of wool and linen combined,
Such mixtures, the Lord doth bind.

Upon your garments, fringes make,
On four corners, a command to partake.
These tassels shall remind you true,
Of God's laws and what you should do.

If a man takes a wife but hates her so,
Bringing evil charges, deceit to sow,
The tokens of virginity he disclaims,
Before elders, her innocence reclaims.

The father and mother shall present,
Proof of virginity, to prevent,
False charges, evil names on her cast,
Before the city's elders, it's steadfast.

If proven false, a fine they impose,
One hundred shekels, as justice shows.
For evil speech upon a pure soul,
A man shall pay, to make her whole.

But if true, the tokens not there,
A damsel in folly, caught in a snare,
Before her father's door, she shall die,
Stoned by the city, the law applied.

If a man lies with a married wife,
Both shall perish, forfeiting life.
Evil thus expelled from the land,
Justice upheld by God's command.

If a virgin is betrothed in the town,
And with a man she's found lying down,
Both to the gate, they shall lead,
Stoning them, their lives to cede.

But if in the field the act is done,
Only the man shall meet the sun.
The damsel is innocent in this case,
As helpless as one in a deathly chase.

If a virgin not betrothed is found,
Lying with a man on the ground,
Fifty shekels he must pay,
And marry her, not turn away.

A man must not his father's wife take,
Nor expose his father's honor for his sake.

GUARDING AGAINST WICKEDNESS

Listen closely now, I've got to say,
If a man's been hurt in a certain way,
His private parts wounded, or cut off, you see,
God's congregation he won't enter, it's a decree.

A bastard child, too, has a certain fate,
No entry to God's congregation, it's straight.
For ten generations, they must wait outside,
Before they can join, with no secrets to hide.

Ammonites and Moabites, they're not in our grace,
Till their tenth generation, they'll find no place.
They withheld bread and water, back in the day,
As we left Egypt's land and made our way.

They hired Balaam to curse, to cause us pain,
But God turned the curse to blessings, without restrain.
Though they stood against us, God's love held sway,
And blessings were granted, leading us on our way.

So, don't seek their peace or their prosperity,
These nations are separate, that's how it should be.
But don't abhor an Edomite, they're kin, you see,
And don't shun an Egyptian, remember, you were free.

Their children, third generation, can find a place,
In God's congregation, they'll join the race.
When we go to battle, avoid wicked things,
Keep your hearts pure, and let virtue take wings.

If someone's unclean at night, here's the deal,
They must leave the camp, the uncleanness to heal.
Wash with water at evening's close, it's the way,
Rejoin the camp when the sun ends the day.

There's a spot outside the camp, you should know,
For your private needs, it's where you can go.
A tool in your hand, for a task discreet,
To bury waste, keep the camp clean and neat.

Remember, God walks among us, it's true,
In our midst, delivering us from what we rue.
Keep the camp holy, free from impurity,
God's presence among us, a sacred security.

A servant escaped from another's hold,
Don't return them, let their freedom unfold.
Let them dwell with you, treat them fair,
No oppression or mistreatment, it's only fair.

No harlotry, no immoral ways to tread,
In Israel, let righteousness be spread.
No offerings tainted, no earnings from sin,
God's house should be pure, let virtue begin.

Lending with usury, towards a kin, take heed,
Be it money or goods, it's a sensitive creed.
But to a stranger, you can lend with a hand,
For blessings from God, on you, they'll land.

When you make a vow to God, don't delay,
Fulfill it promptly, don't let it sway.
Your words are important, a promise to keep,
Freewill offerings, let your commitments run deep.

In your neighbor's vineyard, feel free to partake,
Grapes to enjoy, a treat you can make.
In standing corn, gently gather what's fair,
Respect your neighbor's crops, treat them with care.

SHARING THE HARVEST

Listen closely now, my friend, I say,
When wedded ties begin to fray,
And love's once-bright flame starts to dim,
Know there's a way to part and trim.

If in her ways you find some flaw,
A bill of divorce you can draw,
Place it within her gentle hand,
And free her to another land.

Once out of your house, she's unbound,
With another love, she may be found.
But if that new love turns to hate,
Or death befalls, sealing her fate,

To you, her first, she can't return,
For that would cause the land to burn.
Remember this, let it be known,
Inheritance's seed shall be sown.

When a new spouse you take in tow,
No wars you fight, no battles know.
A year of joy at home you'll share,
With your new bride, love's tender care.

No millstone's use as a pledge's plight,
For that could bring eternal night.
Stealing kin or making them merchandise,
Demands a death, let justice rise.

Leprosy's mark, beware its sign,
The priests will guide, their wisdom fine.
Think of Miriam, her tale hold dear,
As Egypt's chains we all did bear.

When lending help to kin in need,
Stay outside, don't intercede.
Let pledges rest within their space,
Return them at dusk, honor's embrace.

For those in labor, poor and weak,
Wages due, their hearts do seek.
Before the sun sets on that day,
Pay what you owe without delay.

Remember, each soul accounts for its sin,
Fathers not for sons, let justice win.
Strangers, orphans, widows, too,
Uphold their rights, let kindness ensue.

In Egypt's past, we were confined,
God's mercy and love forever bind.
Leave gleanings in fields and vineyards tall,
For strangers, orphans, heed this call.

Think of your servitude, your past,
Injustice is a die we cast.
With compassion's light, let justice shine,
In every action, make God's will align.

EQUITABLE MEASURES

When disputes arise and judgment's near,
The judges shall discern what's clear.
Righteousness they'll favor, evil they'll condemn,
In the courtroom, fairness is their gem.

For the wicked deserving of a painful blow,
A limited count of lashes, not to overflow.
No more than forty, to preserve their pride,
Lest his dignity and worth subside.

The ox that treads the corn, let it be,
No muzzle to stifle, let it roam free.
If brothers dwelling, one meets his end,
A widow's path, let compassion mend.

The brother-in-law, his duty shall heed,
To honor the lost, a sacred deed.
The firstborn's name, he shall carry on,
Their legacy lives, their memory won't be gone.

If the brother declines, the task he fears,
The widow shall act, she won't shed tears.
His shoe she'll remove, a symbol, a sign,
His choice to decline, his legacy's decline.

In the midst of conflict, a woman's hand,
To rescue her husband, her brave stand.
But if she grasps where she should not dare,
Her hand shall be lost, a lesson rare.

Weights and measures, honest and straight,
No cheating or tricks, let fairness be your trait.
A perfect scale, an honest cup,
In God's land of blessings, hold your trust up.

Unrighteousness, God's eyes despise,
Abominable acts under His skies.
Amalek's cruelty, remember that day,
When leaving Egypt's shadows gray.

Striking the weak, the weary, the frail,
No fear of God, their hearts did fail.
Rest from enemies, a gift ahead,
Amalek's stain, let it be shed.

Erase their memory, blot out their name,
From the annals of time, wipe away their shame.
In the land of promise, where justice finds its place,
Remember God's mercy, embrace His grace.

HAND OF GOD

In the land you'll soon possess,
Where God's blessings freely bless,
Take the first fruits of your land,
In a basket, humbly stand.

Bring them to the chosen place,
Where God's name holds honored space,
Tell the priest with joyful heart,
"We've reached the land, a brand new start."

Before God's altar, set them down,
A symbol of blessings that abound,
Speak aloud, let it be heard,
"Our forefather was once unheard."

From a foreign land he came,
Egypt's hardship, grief, and pain,
Though few, he grew and thrived,
In oppression, hope survived.

The Egyptians treated us unkind,
But God's grace, our hearts did find,
He saw our plight, reached out His hand,
Led us from Egypt's cruel land.

With mighty signs and wonders true,
God's power shown to guide us through,
To this land, a land so fair,
Flowing with milk and honey's share.

Stand before God, your gratitude show,
Before His altar, humbly bow,
Tell Him, "I've brought my offering near,
In this land of promise, without fear."

Celebrate His gifts so grand,
In this blessed and fertile land,
For every good thing He bestows,
For the Levite and the stranger, He knows.

When the third year comes around,
Share your tithe on holy ground,
For the Levite, stranger, orphans in need,
God's love through your giving will proceed.

Tell God, "I've done as You've asked,
No part of Your command I've masked,
To the Levite, stranger, and those in despair,
I've given with love and utmost care."

Look down, O God, from heaven's height,
Bless this land with Your guiding light,
As we obey Your commands each day,
In unity, we'll surely stay.

Declare with a heart that's true,
"You are our God, our strength anew,
We'll walk in Your ways, listen to Your voice,
In Your commandments, we'll rejoice."

Above all nations, we'll rise and stand,
A holy people in Your hand,
In praise and honor, our hearts will sing,
As Your chosen ones, we'll bring light to everything.

WRITTEN IN STONE

Listen, people, to this decree,
Moses speaks with wisdom, see,
Keep the commandments, day by day,
As you journey forth, obey.

When you cross Jordan's flowing tide,
On its banks, great stones abide,
Cover them with plaster, clear and bright,
Inscribe God's law, His holy light.

These words of law, forever true,
On these stones, you shall construe,
As you enter a land so grand,
Flowing with milk and honey's hand.

In Mount Ebal's sacred space,
Set up stones in rightful place,
Build an altar, pure and strong,
No iron tool should touch, belong.

Let offerings rise, like incense sweet,
Burnt sacrifices, complete,
With peace offerings, dine and cheer,
Rejoice before God, draw Him near.

Engrave His law on stones with care,
Plain and clear, for all to bear,
Moses and priests proclaim this call,
Obey, O Israel, one and all.

Today, you stand as God's chosen flock,
Obey His voice, like solid rock,
Moses instructs, his voice so clear,
The time to heed is now, no fear.

Upon Mount Gerizim, blessings pour,
From Simeon to Benjamin, adore,
Yet on Mount Ebal, curses found,
From Reuben to Naphtali's ground.

The Levites' voice rings out with might,
Cursed be those who walk in spite,
Making images, straying far,
Disobeying God's righteous bar.

Cursed are those who show disdain,
To father, mother, in cruel gain,
Who move landmarks, wander blind,
Pervert justice, cruel minds.

Cursed are those who sin with lust,
Incest, bestial acts unjust,
Smiting neighbors, taking bribes,
Spilling innocent blood in tribes.

Cursed is the one who won't embrace,
God's holy law, His truth, His grace,
Together, the people declare, "Amen,"
Upholding God's law, again and again.

GROPING IN DARKNESS

Listen up, my friend, I've got to say,
Pay attention now, don't turn away,
If you follow God's commands so true,
Blessings will chase after you.

High above nations, you will soar,
God's favor on you, more and more,
In the city, in the field,
His blessings will be your shield.

Your body, your cattle, your land so wide,
Overflowing blessings, you can't hide,
Coming and going, day by day,
His goodness will light your way.

Enemies will scatter, flee in fear,
God's protection will be clear,
In your storehouses and what you do,
Blessings will come, and they'll renew.

A holy people, set apart,
Following God, with all your heart,
All the nations will see and know,
God's name on you, a radiant glow.

Abundance of goods, in every way,
Rain from heaven, day by day,
Lending to many, borrowing none,
Success and favor, under the sun.

Leading, not lagging, above, not below,
Hold tight to God, and blessings will flow,
Stick to His path, never go astray,
His blessings will guide you, come what may.

But if you stray from His command,
Curses will follow, hard to withstand,
Cursed in the city, cursed in the field,
No escape from the woes revealed.

Diseases, darkness, troubles untold,
Scattered among nations, a story unfolds,
Life in turmoil, no rest in sight,
Longing for relief, day and night.

Return to God, the right way to choose,
Obey His words, don't ever lose,
For in His path, blessings reside,
Walk with Him, by His side.

DESOLATION OF THE LAND

Listen closely now, let me tell,
The covenant words, a story to spell,
Commanded by God through Moses' voice,
A pact to live by, a sacred choice.

Remember the days in Egypt's land,
Pharaoh's grasp, his mighty hand,
Great signs and miracles, all so clear,
But still, some hearts refused to hear.

Forty years in the wilderness wide,
Clothes unaged, shoes by your side,
No bread or wine did you partake,
To know God's presence, for His sake.

Facing Sihon and Og, you fought with might,
Defeating kings in a daring fight,
Their lands were claimed, given as share,
To Reuben, Gad, and Manasseh's heir.

Hold tight to these words, this covenant true,
Obey and prosper in all you do,
All of you stand, young and old,
Before God's presence, bold and bold.

Your tribe leaders, elders so wise,
Officers, all with searching eyes,
Little ones, wives, strangers near,
United in purpose, without fear.

This oath with God, a pact to bind,
To establish His people, heart and mind,
For Abraham, Isaac, Jacob's line,
A promise upheld, divine and fine.

It's not just for you, but those afar,
In Egypt's land, nations bizarre,
Idols and abominations they hold,
Wood and stone, silver and gold.

Beware of turning your hearts away,
To serve other gods, led astray,
A root of bitterness, deep and wide,
Curses unleashed, no place to hide.

When hearing the curse, don't assume,
Peace will follow, dispelling gloom,
God's anger will rise, fierce and strong,
Curses shall follow, all your life long.

Separated for evil, God will decree,
From all the tribes, a destiny,
Future generations, those yet to see,
Shall ask of the land, so barren and free.

A land of brimstone, salt, and flame,
Where nothing grows, it's not the same,
Sodom, Gomorrah's fate you'll share,
An example of God's righteous glare.

All nations will wonder, ask and inquire,
Why such anger, destruction, and fire?
The answer is clear, in the covenant's light,
Forsaking God's ways, brought this plight.

They worshiped gods unknown, untrue,
Angered the Lord, away they flew,
Expelled from their land, in wrath's embrace,
Rooted out, displaced, a solemn trace.

Some mysteries hidden, to God they belong,
But what's revealed, to us does throng,
To follow His laws, with hearts so sure,
In this covenant's truth, forever endure.

ABUNDANCE AND JOY

Listen close, my friend, to what I say,
In the future's sun or cloudy day,
When blessings come or troubles sting,
Remember these words that I bring.

If you find yourself in a distant place,
Lost among nations in life's fast-paced race,
Turn back to God, with heart and soul,
His voice, His ways, your ultimate goal.

He'll gather you up, from near and far,
In His loving embrace, like a shining star,
No matter how distant, no matter how wide,
He'll bring you back, right by His side.

From heaven's heights to lands unknown,
You won't be left to face it alone,
Your fathers' home, a land to possess,
Blessings will flow, in plenty and excess.

He'll touch your heart, make love ignite,
For God, your soul will take flight,
Curses on those who stand in your way,
He'll bless your work, day by day.

Abundance and joy, like a river's flow,
In the fruit of your labor, He'll bestow,
Rejoicing over you, just as before,
He'll shower you with blessings, more and more.

No need to search, no need to roam,
God's words are near, right here at home,
In your heart, on your lips, so plain to see,
His guidance is there, so pure and free.

Life and death, before you laid,
A choice to make, don't be afraid,
Choose the path of love and light,
Obey His voice, in Him take flight.

But if you stray, to idols bow,
Darkness will follow, troubles will plow,
A warning I give, so you may learn,
Turn to God's love, before you yearn.

Earth and sky, they both bear witness,
To life and death, each choice's fitness,
Choose life, my friend, hold love so tight,
In God's embrace, find endless light.

Love Him, obey Him, stand by His side,
For in Him, true life abides,
In the land He promised, you'll find your place,
A legacy of love, by His grace.

WITNESS SONG

Listen closely now to what I say,
Moses' words from long ago, still in display,
At one hundred twenty years, I stand today,
Jordan's banks I won't cross, God's will obey.

The Lord assures, don't fear, don't dread,
He'll go ahead, destroy, make way ahead,
Just like the kings of old, He'll strike them dead,
With Joshua by your side, as He has said.

Sihon, Og, their lands we did reclaim,
Your enemies, too, you won't be in shame,
Obey His words, don't let your courage wane,
God's promise is firm, your path He'll frame.

For Joshua, a charge to lead you strong,
With God beside him, nothing can go wrong,
Fear not, be strong, keep moving along,
His presence with you, a lifelong song.

This law, I penned, for priests to keep,
Deliver it to all, young and old, a promise deep,
Gather the people, in learning steep,
God's words engraved in hearts, a treasure to reap.

A song I leave, a witness to your way,
A warning and guidance, come what may,
In good times and bad, let it light your day,
God's covenant, don't let it slip away.

Joshua, my heir, now take your stand,
Lead Israel to the promised land,
Be strong, be bold, guided by His hand,
God's presence with you, like shifting sand.

The words I wrote, in a book they lie,
Beside the Ark, for all to see and spy,
A testament to truths that won't deny,
When you stray, this truth won't let you fly.

I know your hearts, your ways, your fall,
Even when my voice you no longer call,
Gathered elders, officers, listen to my call,
Heaven and earth, bear witness to all.

In the days ahead, I know what will unfold,
You'll wander off, let your hearts grow cold,
Evil will find you, as your hearts turn bold,
My words are here, my warning, behold.

So take heed of my song, my friend, my kin,
A solemn reminder of where to begin,
Moses' voice echoes, a guide from within,
Stay true to His covenant, in victory or in sin.

FORGETTING THE ROCK

Listen heavens, and lend an ear,
Earth, pay attention, my words are clear.
Like rain, my teachings fall, like dew they steer,
On tender plants and grass, they now appear.

I'm here to make the name of the Lord known,
Give glory to our God, on His throne.
He's solid as a rock, His ways are shown,
Just, true, and righteous, on His path we're sown.

They went astray, their ways got twisted,
A crooked generation, they existed.
Foolish people, their ways were resisted,
Turn back to God, and be assisted.

Remember days gone by, those years of old,
Seek wisdom from your elders, as we're told.
When nations were divided, stories unfold,
God chose His people, a tale of gold.

In deserts wild, God's care was sweet,
He led them right, their needs to meet.
Like eagles guarding nests, a love complete,
With them alone, His guidance did they greet.

God nourished them with bounties rare,
Honey from rocks, His love to share.
Milk and butter, His kindness to declare,
But they turned away, their hearts did tear.

Idols they embraced, His anger grew,
Sacrificed to demons, all they knew.
They forgot their Rock, and so they slew,
God's wrath ignited, a fate they drew.

A fiery anger, a burning blaze,
Arrows, troubles, in darkened days.
Hunger, swords, in many ways,
God's judgment came, a fearful phase.

Scattered they'll be, forgotten and lost,
God's fury upon them, a terrible cost.
Their wisdom flawed, understanding tossed,
If only they'd see, count what was lost.

How could one chase a thousand, or two, ten?
Without God's might, they'd fail again.
Grapes of bitterness, like poison, then,
Their rock's not like ours, the truth is plain.

Stored up is vengeance, sealed and kept,
A day of reckoning, when all debts are swept.
God's judgment sure, no secrets are left,
He's the only God, on Him, we're kept.

So heed these words, my friend, my kin,
Treasure them close, let them soak in.
Choose life, choose God, let your days begin,
Follow His ways, free from the grip of sin.

And Moses spoke, the song complete,
To Hoshea's ears, a message sweet.
His words were done, a promise to meet,
Guidance and wisdom, for your life's feat.

Set these words in your heart, so they're near,
They're not empty, they're what you should revere.
Live by them now, let their wisdom appear,
Onward in your journey, without fear.

Moses stood on Mount Nebo high,
Canaan's land before him, reaching the sky.
But he wouldn't enter, though he'd try,
His end drew near, he'd bid goodbye.

At Meribah-Kadesh, he faltered, it's true,
Didn't honor God, as we're meant to do.
He glimpsed the land, his time was through,
A lesson learned, for me and for you.

STRENGTH AND BLESSINGS

Listen, all you people, hear my voice,
Moses' blessing, a tale of choice.
From Sinai's heights, God's law did gleam,
Seir, Paran, a divine dream.

With saints in multitude, He came,
A fiery law, His righteous claim.
He loved His people, held them tight,
Under His care, in His holy light.

Moses gave us laws to follow,
Inheritance for Jacob to hallow.
In Jeshurun, a king, he stood,
Guiding the tribes, doing what's good.

Reuben, live and thrive, be strong,
May your numbers grow, a lasting song.
Judah's blessing, Lord, heed his call,
Grant him strength to conquer all.

Levi, you have the Thummim's grace,
Urim's guidance, in every place.
Teaching God's judgments, sacrifices true,
Honor their work, for their faith is due.

Benjamin, safe under God's wing,
His protection, a blessed thing.
Joseph's land, rich and blessed,
From heaven's treasures, truly impressed.

Zebulun, Issachar, rejoice with glee,
Calling people to the mount, you'll be.
Gad, like a lion, fierce and bold,
Justice in God's name, a story told.

Dan, a lion's whelp, he shall leap,
Naphtali, favored, blessings deep.
Asher, blessed with children and more,
Foot dipped in oil, abundance's store.

Shoes of iron, strength to endure,
God of Jeshurun, forever sure.
Eternal refuge, arms embracing,
Defeat the foe, with power amazing.

Israel, dwell in safety's hold,
Jacob's fountain, blessings untold.
Happy are you, saved by the Lord,
With shield and sword, your foes ignored.

None like God, who rides the sky,
Eternal arms, enemies deny.
Israel, victorious, shall stand,
Treading on high places, across the land.

HIDDEN TOMB

Moses climbed to Nebo's height,
From Moab's plains, a splendid sight.
Pisgah's peak, facing Jericho's wall,
God's land revealed, from Gilead to all.

From Dan to Gilead, and Ephraim's land,
Naphtali, Manasseh, and Judah's strand,
From south to plain, where palm trees grow,
Zoar's edge, where waters flow.

God spoke to him, "This land I swore,
To Abraham, Isaac, Jacob of yore.
Though you see it, you won't cross this line,
To your seed, the promise is thine."

Moses, God's servant, met his end,
In Moab's land, His word did send.
Buried in a valley, his tomb concealed,
Bethpeor's sight, a secret revealed.

At a hundred and twenty, strong and clear,
No dimming eye, no weakening fear.
Israel mourned him, thirty days in woe,
Then their tears ceased, and they let him go.

Joshua, wise, the spirit did fill,
Moses' hands on him, a leader's skill.
Israel heeded, followed God's decree,
As Moses directed, as it was meant to be.

A prophet like Moses never rose,
Face to face with God, a friendship close.
In Egypt's land, with signs and might,
He showed God's glory, in wondrous sight.

Mighty hand and great awe he displayed,
Before all Israel, his strength conveyed.
Moses, a beacon, a leader so grand,
Guiding God's people, through desert sand.

Also in the
Threads of Revelation Series:

Pillar of Fire:
Toward the Promised Land

Dawn of Eternity
Edens Legacy Unraveled

Hi. I hope you have enjoyed this book. If you have a moment to spare, I would greatly appreciate it if you could take the time to review it.

If you gained valuable insights, or if your spiritual journey was influenced in any way, I would love to hear about it. Your opinion matters to me and I would be grateful if you could share your experience and thoughts by leaving a review.

www.ingramcontent.com/pod-product-compliance
Lightning Source LLC
Chambersburg PA
CBHW072003040426
42447CB00009B/1463